KOREA
ENVIRONMENTAL
TECHNOLOGIES
EXPORT MARKET PLAN

US-AEP

U.S. DEPARTMENT OF COMMERCE
International Trade Administration
and
United States-Asia Environmental Partnership
Washington, D.C.
July 2002

Library of Congress Cataloging-in-Publication Data

Korea environmental technologies export market plan.
    p. cm.
    1. Pollution control industry   Korea (South) 2. Hazardous waste management industry
Korea (South) 3. Refuse disposal industry   Korea (South) 4. Recycling industry   Korea
(South) 5. Environmental engineering   Korea (South) 6. Exports   Korea (South). I.
United States. International Trade Administration. II. United States. Asia Environmental
Partnership.

HD9718.K62 K67 2001
382'.456285'095195   dc21   2001039781

Map on page vii courtesy of the Central Intelligence Agency.

The full text of this report is available on the International Trade Administration's Internet
site at *www.environment.ita.doc.gov.* Paper or microfiche copies are available for
purchase from the National Technical Information Service, 5285 Port Royal Road,
Springfield, VA 22161; *www.ntis.gov.*

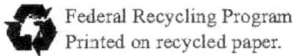

Acknowledgments

This report was produced for the U.S. Department of Commerce through the cooperative efforts of the International Trade Administration's Office of Environmental Technologies Industries and the U.S. and Foreign Commercial Service.

A special thanks goes to the USAID-led interagency program called the US-Asia Environmental Partnership for their support and contributions.

Contents

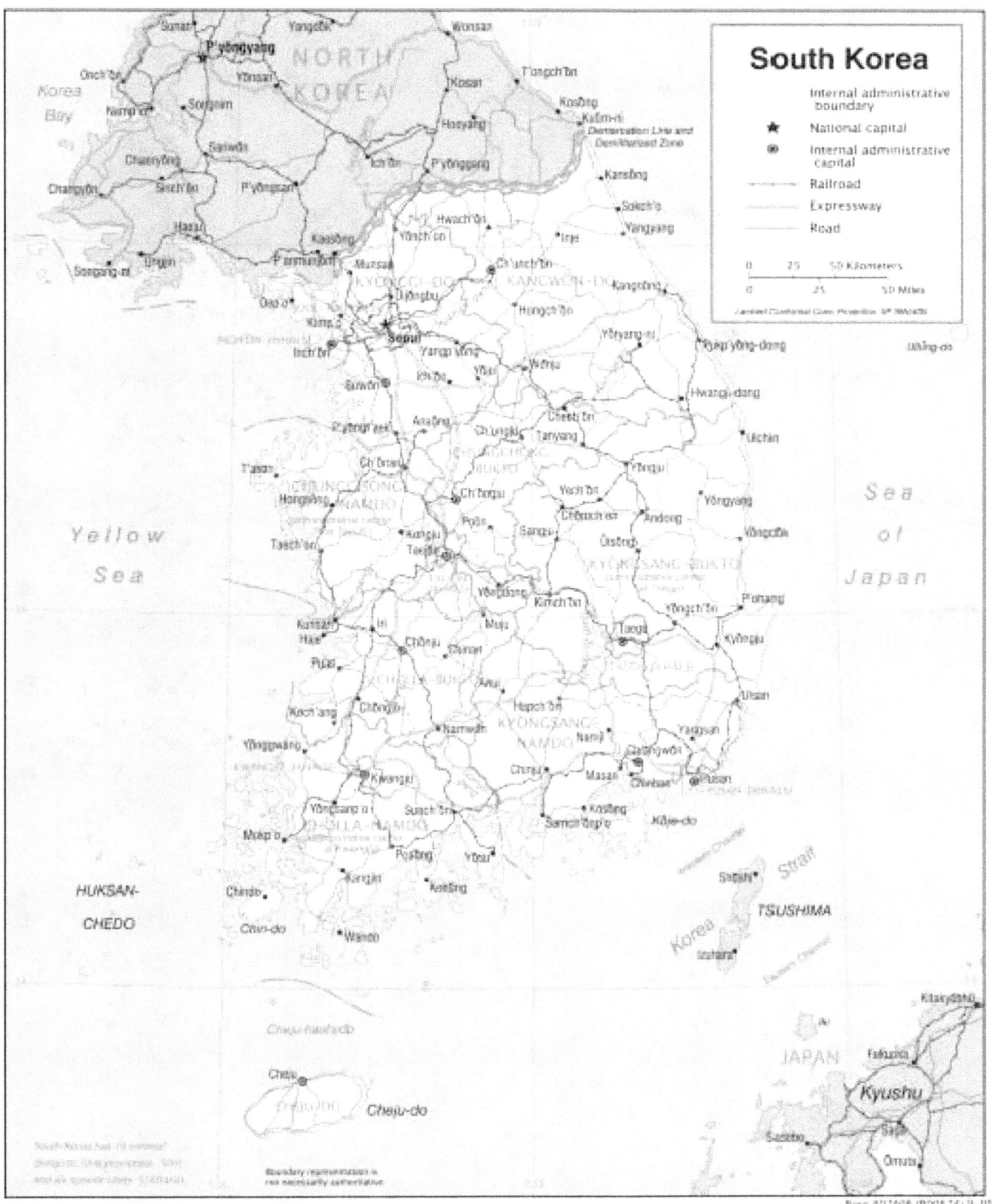

Abbreviations and Acronyms

BOD	biochemical oxygen demand		MOCIE	Ministry of Commerce, Industry, and Energy
CNG	compressed natural gas		MOE	Ministry of Environment
EIA	environmental impact assessment		NIER	National Institute of Environmental Research
EMO	Environmental Management Office			
ECP	Environmental Preservation Committee		NGO	non-governmental organization
FDI	foreign direct investment		OECD	Organization for Economic Cooperation and Development
GDP	gross domestic product			
KEIA	Korea Environmental Industry Association		ppm	parts per million
KEPA	Korea Environmental Preservation Act		R&D	research and development
kg	kilogram		TMS	telemetering system
KORECA	Korea Resources, Recovery, and Reutilization Corporation		TRI	toxic release inventory
			VOC	volatile organic compounds
KrW	Korean won		WHO	World Health Organization
LEMO	Local Environmental Management Office			
m³	cubic meter			

m^3 = cubic meter

Note: Dollar figures given in the report are U.S. dollars. Unless otherwise noted, an exchange rate of 1,100 Korean won per U.S. dollar was used in calculations.

Executive Summary

Korea is one of the largest markets for environmental products and technology in the Asia-Pacific region, with a total size of approximately $7.1 billion in 1999.[1] In the 1990s, Korea's environmental market grew at an annual average of around 16 percent, until 1997, when the financial and economic crisis hit the nation hard. In 1999, the market regained its growth as the national economy bounced back from the economic downturn, and it is expected to reach $7.7 billion in 2000.

Government spending on environmental investment and management totaled $3.9 billion in 1999, up approximately 7 percent from $3.7 billion in 1998, as the government continued to increase investment in environmental infrastructure, including sewage systems and solid waste treatment facilities. The private sector's total environmental spending increased around 9 percent to reach $3.2 billion in 1999, due largely to the enforcement of more demanding regulations for air quality preservation, beginning in January 1999.

Korea's environmental market has expanded under the Korean government's push to improve the nation's environmental quality, which had deteriorated significantly during the previous several decades of rapid industrialization and urbanization. The Korean government's current environmental betterment drive is based on its "Green Vision 21," a long-term environmental master plan for 1996 through 2005, and the revised second mid-term comprehensive plan for 1998 through 2002. Under the mid-term plan, the Korean government is undertaking 141 infrastructure projects with a total investment of $31 billion, the great majority of which were set aside for these sub-sectors: water quality ($13.0 billion), air quality ($8.3 billion), water supply ($5.6 billion), and solid waste treatment ($3.3 billion).

In spite of large investments in environmental infrastructure construction and the strengthened enforcement of regulations, Korea's general environmental quality does not meet the public's needs, particularly drinking water and air quality. The government will continue to expand infrastructure investments in the water and wastewater sub-sectors and in solid waste treatment and to increase enforcement efforts in all sub-sectors of private industry, including industrial waste and wastewater treatment, air pollution abatement, and energy conservation and recovery.

Korean engineering and construction companies, which have relied heavily on foreign engineering technologies and equipment, have traditionally dominated the environmental market. Japanese companies remain the most important foreign player in Korea's market for environmental products and technology due to their geographical and cultural proximity and cost advantage. In recent years, however, U.S. and European environmental companies have increased their business activities and market shares, primarily by penetrating the top end of the market. While Korean engineering and equipment suppliers have upgraded their technological capabilities, they still rely on foreign sources for sophisticated environmental products and services.

For U.S. environmental companies, the Korean market offers greater entry and growth opportunities in various fields. Korean environmental authorities have recently adopted privatization programs for some infrastructure projects, with the likelihood of further privatization in the waste and wastewater treatment sub-sectors, due to increasing need for investment that the government cannot meet. In addition, ongoing public sector reform will require private industries to expand their participation in environmental infrastructure construction and operation. These realities, coupled with the government's accelerated efforts to attract foreign capital, mean expanded opportunities for U.S. environmental engineering and service companies as well as greater need for equipment and components.

Through the next several years, the Korean environmental market is projected to grow at an annual average of approximately 10 percent. Most of this market growth will be registered in the private sector as the government places more emphasis on pollution prevention or reduction, reuse, recycling, and energy recovery rather than

---

1. This figure came from an October 25, 2000, press release from the Bank of Korea, entitled "1999 Environmental Expenditure (Preliminary)." An average exchange rate of 1,100 Korean won per U.S. dollar is used for the currency conversion throughout this report, except where indicated otherwise.

public treatment such as landfill and incineration. But the government will also continue to construct new treatment and monitoring facilities and expand or upgrade existing facilities, many of which are woefully inadequate. Until the 1990s, the growth of Korea's environmental market was driven by the increasing demand for infrastructure construction and related environmental equipment and machinery. In the 2000s, the demand for advanced engineering and other services, such as consulting, cleanup, restoration, and recycling, will grow at a much faster pace than for conventional end-of-pipe fields.

In order to take full advantage of market opportunities and to outperform Japanese and European competitors in the Korean environmental market, U.S. companies should increase market development and promotion. In addition, identifying a capable and trustworthy local partner will be integral to sustainable growth and long-term success in this dynamic and challenging market.

Chapter 1
Economic Overview

By major economic indicators, the Korean economy has apparently been bouncing back since early 1999 from the Asian crisis that hit the nation in late 1997. Korea's GDP grew 10.7 percent in real terms based on the Korean won in 1999 after it dropped 5.7 percent in 1998 on the same basis. In 1999, the manufacturing sector, which accounts for 31.8 percent of the nation's total output, grew 21.8 percent, but the construction sector declined 10.1 percent. In the same year, facility investment and consumer spending increased 38.0 percent and 10.3 percent, respectively.

In the first half of 2000, GDP grew 11.1 percent over the same period a year ago, when it rose 8.2 percent. The dual engine of consumer spending and facility investment powered the robust growth, which rose 10.1 percent and 46.8 percent, respectively. But construction investment shrunk 5.7 percent due to stagnant housing construction and infrastructure investment. Although Korea already may have passed the peak of the current growth cycle, the Ministry of Finance and Economy projects a GDP growth of 8 percent for 2000.

Both merchandise exports and imports have grown significantly since 1999. On a customs clearance basis, exports grew 8.6 percent to reach $143.7 billion in 1999 and 25.5 percent in the first half of 2000 on a year-on-year basis. Imports grew at higher rates of 28.4 percent to reach $119.8 billion in 1999 and 44.7 percent in the same period of 2000. Korea is one of the United States' biggest trading partners. Currently, it is the sixth largest export market for the United States. For Korea, the United States was the largest source of imports with a share of 21.9 percent of total imports in 1999, closely followed by Japan with a 20.2 percent share. In 1999, imports from the U.S. into Korea were $24.9 billion, compared with $20.4 billion in 1998 and $30.0 billion in 1997.

Exports hit a monthly record of $15.5 billion in June 2000. Semiconductors, computers, and petrochemicals largely led this performance. Imports rose to $13.2 billion in the same month due to increasing demand for raw materials and components used in Korea's major industries including semiconductors, computers, telecommunications, automobiles, steel, petrochemicals, textiles,

and machinery. Overall, the country recorded a trade surplus of $4.4 billion in the first half of 2000, far less than the $11.7 billion surplus it achieved a year earlier. The government's target in trade surplus is set at $10 billion for 2000. The nation's foreign reserves hold steady at around $90 billion, thanks to the trade surplus.

Other key economic indicators for the first half of 2000 appear to remain stable. The Korean won has not fluctuated much since it was stabilized at a won 1,100 to won 1,150 against the U.S. dollar in the early half of 2000. In May 2000, the unemployment rate fell to 3.7 percent or 828,000 persons, down from 6.8 percent in 1998 and 6.3 percent in 1999. The consumer price index remained at a healthy rate of 1.5 percent in the first half of 2000 and 0.8 percent in 1999, allowing the government to hold interest rates steady. The benchmark three-year corporate bond rate floated below 10 percent in the first half of 2000. Many economists, however, expect inflation to accelerate to about 3 percent by the year-end. The current favorable economic circumstances will likely worsen in the remaining period of 2000 and 2001 as the business cycle begins to reverse, according to a recent report released by the Korea Development Institute, the state-funded think tank.

Foreign inward direct investment has increased remarkably since 1997 due to the Korean government's strong drive to attract foreign capital and the ample opportunities for foreign investors to take over Korean-owned or joint venture companies amid industry and corporate restructuring during the economic crisis. Foreign direct investment (FDI) increased 75.6 percent to a record $15.5 billion in 1999 and further grew 20 percent in the first half of 2000 over the same period of 1999.

The Korean government maintained the expansionary policy stance adopted in mid-1998 to stimulate the economy. It was initially planned to increase the budget by 5 to 6 percent of GDP. The government doubled the budget during the 1999 fiscal year. As a result, fiscal expenditure increased by 9.7 percent above the 1998 level, which itself exceeded the 1997 level by 13.5 percent. Main contributors to the expansion were support for banking and corporate reform, strengthening of social safety nets, and increased investment in infrastructure.

Nevertheless, the rapid recovery enabled the government to reduce the fiscal deficit to 2.9 percent of GDP for the year.

In 1999 and 2000, with significant financial assistance from multilateral development finance institutions, the Republic of Korea has made considerable progress in reforming and restructuring the domestic banking and corporate sectors. In the banking sector, many nonviable financial institutions have been closed, viable institutions have been re-capitalized, regulations and supervision have been strengthened, and information disclosure and transparency standards have been improved.

The government's corporate restructuring program focused on restructuring corporate finance and improving standards of corporate governance. Debt-to-equity ratios of most large conglomerates have been reduced, and more than 87 percent of the cross-guarantees between the affiliates of the top 30 conglomerates have been phased out. Rights of minority shareholders in companies have been strengthened, and conglomerates are now required to present consolidated financial statements. In summary, substantial progress has been attained in implementing reforms in the finance and corporate sectors. However, many economists urge that the government should accelerate banking and corporate restructuring efforts in order for the national economy to emerge as a fully restructured, sustainable, and truly advanced one.

Table 1.1. Major Korean Economic Indicators

	1997	1998	1999
GDP, current prices (billions of U.S. dollars)	476.6	317.7	406.7
GDP real growth based on Korean won (percent)	5.0	-6.7	10.7
GNI, current prices (billions of U.S. dollars)	474.0	313.0	402.1
GNI real growth based on Korean won (percent)	2.1	-8.8	8.9
Per capita GNI (in U.S. dollars)	10,307	6,742	8,581
Average exchange rate (won to U.S. dollars)	951.1	1,398.9	1,189.5
Unemployment rate (percent)	2.6	6.8	6.3
Producer price inflation (percent)	3.9	12.2	-2.1
Consumer price inflation (percent)	4.5	7.5	0.8
Interest rate (three-year corporate bond yield) (percent)	13.39	14.99	8.86
Current account balance (billions of U.S. dollars)	-8.2	40.0	25.0
Foreign currency reserves	19.7	52.0	73.7
Total exports (billions of U.S. dollars)	136	133	144
Total imports (billions of U.S. dollars)	145	93	120
Exports to U.S. (billions of U.S. dollars)	21.6	22.8	29.5
Imports from U.S. (billions of U.S. dollars)	30.0	20.4	24.9
Foreign direct investment (millions of U.S. dollars)	6,971	8,852	15,541
FDI from U.S. (millions of U.S. dollars)	3,190	2,973	3,738
FDI from E.U. (millions of U.S. dollars)	2,409	2,968	6,423
FDI from Japan (millions of U.S. dollars)	266	504	1,750

Source: National Statistical Office, Bank of Korea, Ministry of Finance and Economy.

Chapter 2
Overview of the Korean Market for Environmental Technologies

Korea has a relatively short history of environmental protection compared with major advanced nations such as the United States and the European countries. While the environmental industry emerged in the 1970s, environmental concerns gave way to rapid economic development, industrialization, and urbanization. For example, in the latter part of the 1970s, serious pollution problems arose around the Ulsan Industrial Complex, one of the major industrial areas in Korea. With the passage of the Environmental Preservation Act of 1977, the environmental market started to grow. In the 1980s, environmental problems grew more serious on a number of fronts as industrialization advanced rapidly. As a result, in 1980, the law was categorized to cover air, water, noise and vibration, hazardous substances, and environmental dispute settlement. As new environmental issues emerged, new laws followed. Currently, the Ministry of Environment directly executes 30 laws.

Market Opportunities and Potential

Korea's environmental industry consists of 17 business categories and approximately 12,400 companies. Based on environmental spending data released by the Bank of Korea, the nation's central bank, the environmental market had expanded at an annual average of 15 to 17 percent since 1990 to reach $7.7 billion in 1997, but the market shrunk to $6.6 billion in 1998 during the financial and economic crisis that started in late 1997. In 1999, the market grew 7.8 percent over the previous year to $7.1 billion. In 1999, the government spent $3.9 billion, representing 55 percent of Korea's total environmental expenditure, on environmental infrastructure construction and management, while the private sector spent $3.2 billion (45 percent) on environmental investment and management, of which $2.9 billion (40.7 percent) was spent by industry and $0.3 billion (4.3 percent) by households. In 2000, Korea's total environmental market is expected to grow approximately 7 percent to $7.7 billion.

In general, Korea lags far behind major advanced nations in its technological capability, largely due to its short history of environmental management and incapability to develop basic environmental technologies. Thus, the environmental industry has largely depended on foreign sources, mainly Japan, the United States, Germany, and other European countries. The Ministry of Environment (MOE) generally assesses the nation's overall level of environmental technology in the range of 30 to 70 percent of the most advanced level.[1]

As a result of concerted public and private efforts to improve and localize environmental technology, Korean companies in traditional "end-of-the pipe" fields, such as effluent and wastewater treatment and hazardous waste treatment, have developed their own technologies. Some leading companies also recently have started commercializing such technologies as dust filtration and desulfurization. Nonetheless, the industry as a whole still depends heavily on foreign sources of technology in the fields of engineering of core equipment and engineering/production of core parts. Most private environmental companies still tend to prefer adopting foreign technology, rather than developing original technology, when they conduct projects or produce equipment. In addition, Korea's efforts to develop environmental technology are still focused on engineering and construction involving environmental infrastructure projects, such as municipal wastewater treatment plants and incinerators. Korea still remains at its infancy in more advanced fields, such as cleanup, recovery, and recycling, which will lead the market for environmental technologies in the 21st century.

Since 1992, the Ministry of Environment has implemented a private-public joint research and development program to upgrade Korea's environmental technology. Between 1992 and 1998, a total of over $300 million was spent under this program. As a result, 154 research and development (R&D) projects were completed and 294

---

1. A 1997 publication released by the state-run Korea Institute of Science and Technology (KIST) evaluated the level of Korea's environmental technology by sub-sector relative to most advanced nations, as follows: air 30–70 percent; water/wastewater 30–60 percent; solid waste 20–60 percent; soil and ground water 30–50 percent; environmental cleanup 20–30 percent; global environmental management 30–50 percent; marine environment 20–30 percent; ecology 10–20 percent; and environmental preservation 10–30 percent.

projects were in progress as of the end of 1999. Since 1998, 140 projects have been conducted with an emphasis on commercializing the environmental technologies already developed through this program. The Ministry of Commerce, Industry, and Energy (MOCIE) has also initiated and pursued environmental R&D programs in such fields as clean energy and clean manufacturing.

The General State of the Environment

The environment has become a core component in determining a nation's international competitiveness as well as the level of national welfare. Koreans are increasingly conscious of environmental issues directly affecting their quality of life. At the same time, international pressures to preserve the global environment are accelerating. Even though the major advanced nations and international organizations call for institutionalizing higher standards of environmental protection on a global basis, the current state of environmental management in Korea does not seem to have effectively met the public's need for a better environment. Air quality in the ozone layer continues to deteriorate in major urban areas, and water quality in the major water resources is still far less than what people desire even as the number of polluting sources continues to increase. From the standard of major advanced nations, Korea still lacks environmental infrastructures such as wastewater and solid waste treatment facilities. In addition, land development policy has not been pursued in a way to properly preserve the environment.

Environmental Investment Incentives

The Korean government offers two types of environmental investment incentives to industries: tax incentives and low-interest loans. First, the government grants customs-duty reductions or exemptions on pollution control equipment imports. In 1998, for instance, the government granted 93 cases of duty reduction or exemption with a total of $195 million. Second, the government offers long-term, low-interest loans to environmental investors and technology developers. Also, in 1998, the government granted low-interest loans for 1,040 environmental projects.

Near and Medium-Term Environmental Priorities

In April 1999, the Korean government confirmed the revised Second Mid-Term Comprehensive Plan for Environmental Improvement for 1998 to 2002. The original plan was established and confirmed in April 1997. As a result of the 1997 Asian economic crisis, the government revised the original plan to reflect the changing economic outlook. Despite the economic crisis, the government did expand the environmental budget and the number of projects in its revised plan, reflecting the government's strong willingness to preserve the environment.

Under the revised second mid-term environmental plan, the government plans to initiate 141 infrastructure projects with a total budget of $33.2 billion for 1998 through 2002. Of the total budget, $23.9 billion is planned to come from the public fund, and $9.3 billion from the private sector. In the first mid-term (1992–1996), a total of $13.6 billion was invested in 117 projects.

The planned infrastructure investment for each subsector in the second mid-term (1998–2002) is:

Air quality preservation	$8.9 billion
Water quality preservation	$13.9 billion
Water supply management	$6.0 billion
Waste management	$3.5 billion

The second mid-term comprehensive plan is regarded as an action plan for "Green Vision 21," a long-term master plan for national environmental preservation for 1996–2005. The environmental plan is based on five strategic principles:

1. Take "preventive," rather than reactive, measures before pollution or environmental damage occurs.
2. Seek a balance between land development and environmental preservation.
3. Adopt a "polluters pay" principle.
4. Actively use economic incentives to encourage people to voluntarily make efforts to improve the environment.
5. Ensure transparency and public trust on environmental policy planning and implementation by sharing environmental information with the public and encouraging the public's commitment to environmental issues.

Under "Green Vision 21," the government made these issues policy priorities:

- Clean water and sufficient water supply
- Cleaner air
- Recycling and reuse of waste
- Managing safety with chemical pollutants
- Preservation of the natural environment
- Strengthening international cooperation

Key Driving Forces

With the population approaching 47 million and a land area of merely 99,408 square kilometers, Korea has inherent problems in managing environmental issues. The rapid pace of industrialization and urbanization over the past four decades or so has further aggravated the nation's environmental condition in major sub-sectors, including water quality, air quality, solid waste management, and the natural environment. Since the 1980s, the government has increased investment in environmental infrastructure and regulatory efforts to meet the growing demand for a better environment from both the public and the international community.

The Korean environmental industry has grown mainly by localizing foreign technology and products, but Korean engineering firms and equipment manufacturers lack the advanced technology required for modern environmental infrastructure, pollution control equipment, and other environmental devices. Since 1992, both industry and government have made joint efforts to upgrade environmental technology under the G-7 Environmental Engineering and Technology Development Program.

In an effort to expand the demand for the new domestic technology, the government began privatizing environmental infrastructures in 1999 and working toward attracting private capital for selected infrastructure projects. It also aims to develop the environmental industry as a strategic export industry by supporting environmental start-ups and increasing government-industry joint R&D efforts. Future R&D efforts will be focused more on such fields as clean energy, abatement of global warming, low-pollution technologies for automobiles, environmental bio-engineering, hazardous fine chemicals, and measuring devices.

Chapter 3
Legal and Regulatory Review

National and Local Government Entities

The authority and responsibility for environmental issues are shared among the Ministry of Environment, other national government agencies, and local governments.

The Ministry of Environment and Its Subsidiaries

MOE plays the leading role in managing environmental issues on the national level. MOE consists of the Planning and Management Office and six bureaus: Environmental Policy, Nature Conservation, Air Quality Management, Water Quality Management, Water Supply and Sewage Treatment, and Waste Management and Recycling.

MOE subsidiary organizations include the Central Environmental Disputes Coordination Commission, the National Institute of Environmental Research, and four environmental management offices that are responsible for the regions surrounding four major rivers (Han, Nakdong, Keum, and Youngsan). The environmental management offices include four regional environmental management offices and eight environmental branch offices across the nation.

While MOE establishes the framework of environmental policy, including related laws and regulations, the environmental management offices (EMO) and local governments are responsible for implementing policy and regulations. The main role and responsibilities of each office are:

- establishing measures to preserve the environment within its jurisdiction;
- managing polluting establishments in national industrial estates;
- directing and supervising the establishment and operation of environmental infrastructure facilities;
- managing environmental businesses; and
- managing wastes designated by law.

Each regional environmental office conducts the following activities within its jurisdiction:

- assessing environmental impact,
- preserving the natural environment,
- measuring and analyzing environmental pollution, and
- investigating environmental accidents.

Local Governments

Local governments carry out their own environmental mission and those delegated by MOE, including the following activities:

- establishing measures to preserve the local environment;
- collection and disposal of municipal waste;
- disposal of sewage, night soil, and livestock wastewater;
- managing discharging businesses outside of industrial parks; and
- collecting Environmental Improvement Fees.

Each local government has an environmental section in charge of issues within its jurisdiction. The Health and Environmental Research Institutes under the provincial and local governments are responsible for monitoring environmental quality as well as conducting environmental tests and inspections.

Other National Government Agencies

Other national agencies also manage environmental issues.

The Ministry of Science and Technology:

- coordinates nuclear power safety regulations;
- plans and implements protective measures for radioactivity; and
- regulates the transport, treatment, and disposal of nuclear substances and radiation.

The Ministry of Agriculture and Forestry:

- establishes and executes measures to control pollution in the agricultural sector; and
- plans irrigation projects and offers educational programs on irrigation.

The Ministry of Commerce, Industry, and Energy:

- regulates industry's export and import activities concerning toxic substances and importation of industrial waste;
- regulates the planning of industrial site location and the management of industrial parks;
- manages the supply and pollution control of low-sulfuric oil;
- establishes and implements the research and development policy on new or replacement energy; and
- manages safety and pollution control issues involving nuclear power plants and nuclear waste.

The Ministry of Construction and Transportation:

- establishes and coordinates national land development plans;
- designates restricted areas according to the National Land Use Management Act;
- designates areas of restricted development;
- establishes and coordinates national water resource development plans;
- manages rivers and reclamation and temporary use of rivers and lakes;
- enforces type approval and performance test for automobiles; and
- initiates the development of tourist zones.

The Ministry of Labor establishes and executes measures to prevent occupational diseases and to improve work environments.

The Ministry of Culture and Tourism manages the protection of rare species of animals and plants.

The Ministry of Marine Affairs and Fisheries:

- protects fishery resources and establishes measures to control marine and inland water pollution;
- manages reclamation projects and public waters;
- establishes and executes measures to control port pollution; and
- manages marine pollution control issues.

The Forestry Administration:

- establishes basic forestry management policies and plans; and
- manages forest preservation issues.

Legal Framework

Korea's environmental laws are based on Article 35 of the Constitution: "All people have the right to live a life in a healthy and pleasant environment, and the government and the people shall make efforts to conserve the environment."

The formation and development of environmental laws and regulations are closely related to the public's perception of environmental problems. In Korea, environmental concerns emerged in the 1960s when the country began to pursue industrialization. To address these concerns, the Pollution Prevention Act was enacted in 1963. This act lacked effectiveness and practicality in managing complex environmental issues, so it was drastically revised in 1971 to introduce several measures aimed at more effectively managing environmental matters, such as those related to emission standards and the construction of emitting facilities. As rapid industrialization and development continued, public concern about pollution problems surged significantly. In response, in 1977, the Environmental Preservation Act was enacted. It introduced several schemes to cope with environmental problems in a more proactive and comprehensive way as well as to prevent environmental damage or degradation.

In the 1980s, Korea's environmental problems worsened as economic development progressed, giving rise to not one new law but six, which were enacted in 1990. They include the Basic Environmental Policy Act, the Air Quality Preservation Act, the Water Quality Preservation Act, the Noise and Vibration Control Act, the Toxic Chemicals Control Act, and the Environmental Dispute Settlement Act. Since then, a number of other laws have followed, including the Soil Environment Preservation Act, the Drinking Water Act, and the Underground Living Space Air Quality Control Act. Today, the Ministry of Environment is responsible for 30 environmental laws.

Underlying all of these laws is the Basic Environmental Policy Act, which provides the principles and goals of the national environmental preservation policy. Its main content includes the "polluters pay" principle, matters relating to establishing and enforcing the comprehensive long-term environmental preservation plan, and the responsibilities of business establishments that discharge pollutants.

In 1999, MOE streamlined Korea's environmental laws as part of a government deregulation drive. At the same time, MOE introduced new regulations to address problems that arose in enforcing the laws in the past. Other ministries, including the Ministry of Construction and Transportation, the Ministry of Commerce, Industry and Energy, the Ministry of Marine Affairs and Fisheries, the Ministry of Science and Technology, and the Ministry of Agriculture and Forestry, are responsible for the regulations of more than 50 other laws that relate to the environment.

Enforcement Activities and Trends

The Korean government attains its environmental goals mainly through direct regulation and environmental charges. Programs such as the Environmental Impact Assessment and the Environmental Feasibility Review are also used. In addition, MOE operates the Environmental Surveillance Force, which monitors the environmental quality surrounding four major rivers and oversees voluntary environmental management programs for the private sector.

The instruments for direct regulation include creating standards for polluting media, granting approval or permission for discharging facilities, and providing guidance and inspection. In case of violation, environmental authorities can impose penalties in various forms, including improvement order, closure or suspension of operation, business license cancellation, fines, and imprisonment. Installing or upgrading discharging facilities requires MOE's approval or permission as a preventive measure to minimize pollutant emissions. MOE's administrative guidance and inspection involves checking discharging establishments to ensure that they comply with all environmental requirements. The government also employs monetary instruments for environmental management purposes, including the Environmental Improvement Fee, the Emission Fee, the Deposits for Waste Discharge, the Waste Fee, and the Water Quality Improvement Fee.

Enacted in 1993 and amended in 1997, the Environmental Impact Assessment (EIA) Act is currently mandatory for 17 development categories and 62 sub-categories. It requires authorities in charge of project approval to initiate EIA consultation. The developer should comply with all EIA requirements based on the EIA consultation, while the relevant government authorities should monitor and enforce them. The Amendment of

1997 effected more stringent penalties against non-compliance activities. Over the last several years, 150 to 160 cases of EIA consultation were reported each year. The regional environmental management offices initiated 70 percent of all EIA consultations.

Korea has also adopted the Environmental Feasibility Review (EFR) for smaller projects. Like the EIA, the purpose of the EFR is to assess and monitor the environmental impact of development projects. The environmental management offices have initiated the great majority of the EFR cases. Over the last several years, 700 to 1,000 EFR cases were conducted.

Other Environmental Organizations

The Korean government operates 34 environmental commissions that make policy recommendations and review existing policy. The prime minister leads the Environmental Preservation Commission (EPC), which is the highest-level policymaking institution. EPC has 23 members: 14 national government ministers and nine civilians. EPC reviews and resolves medium- and long-term national environmental plans and important environmental issues. The government also operates several councils to discuss policy issues with other sectors including industry, non-governmental environmental organizations, and the military.

Hundreds of non-governmental organizations (NGOs) influence environmental issues. In 1999, 128 NGOs, including major research institutes, industry associations, academic societies, and environmental activist groups, were listed with the Ministry of Environment.

The National Institute of Environmental Research (NIER) is MOE's research hub. NIER is responsible for supporting MOE in creating environmental policy and educating environmental officials. In particular, NIER drafts a variety of environmental standards. NIER consists of five departments, four offices, 17 sections, the Automobile Pollution Research Lab, and four water quality inspection labs. Other influential research institutes include the state-run Korea Institute of Science and Technology, the National Environmental Protection Institute, and the Korea Environment and Technology Institute.

The Korea Environment Preservation Association (KEPA) supports both industry and government by providing various educational, promotional, and research services, including organizing trade shows, seminars, conventions, and educational programs. The Korea Environmental Industry Association (KEIA) represents the interests of pollution control contractors and other envi-

Figure 3.1   Major Environmental Laws of Korea

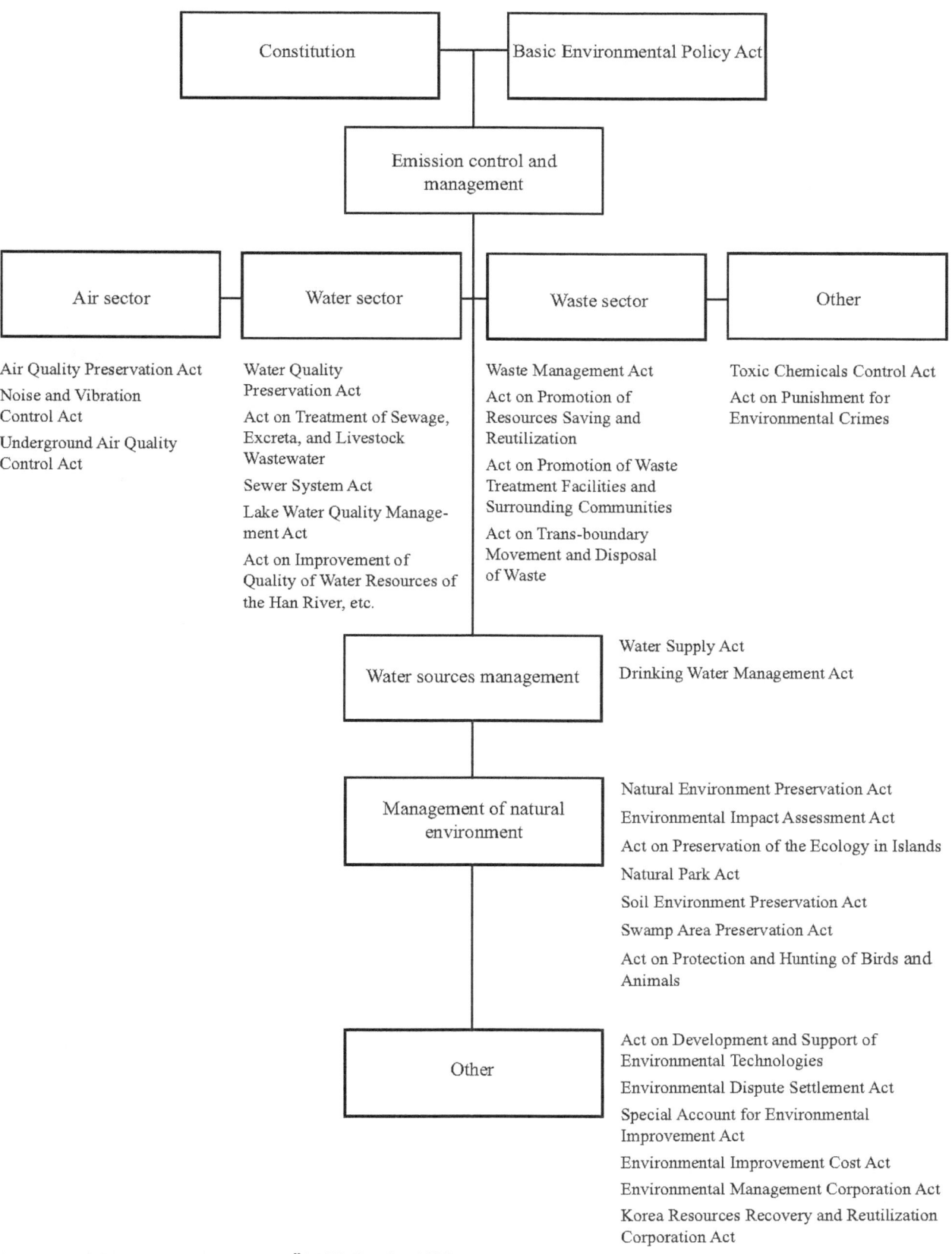

Source: "1999 Environment White Paper," MOE (October 1999).

ronmental businesses. KEIA frequently organizes international cooperation and promotion programs such as trade missions, joint technical seminars, and conventions. KEIA is also building an environment market database as part of MOE's Environmental Technology Information System initiative.

Environmental Management Efforts

Water Quality

In 1996, MOE set up comprehensive measures to manage water quality. Since then, the government has made efforts to improve the nation's water quality, primarily through water and wastewater infrastructure construction and more stringent management of polluting sources. But the results are minimal since the number of polluting sources continues to increase. Municipal water infrastructure should still be expanded in many agricultural areas and islands. The supply of municipal water is 84.5 percent nationwide. But the municipal water supply percentage for Korea's agricultural areas and islands is only 23 percent and 12 percent respectively. In addition, many people do not trust the quality of their tap water in spite of continued government efforts for improvement. To tackle this problem, MOE has conducted in-depth envi-

ronmental research for each of the four major rivers to establish comprehensive measures to improve water quality. MOE has already implemented new policy measures for the Han River, the source of drinking water for Seoul and its surrounding areas.

Air Quality

From the 1960s through the 1980s, Korea's air quality increasingly deteriorated, particularly in industrial areas and large cities. The government's abatement efforts have resulted in reducing such pollutants as sulfurous acid gas, smoke, and particles. But air quality associated with ozone and hazardous air pollutants has deteriorated in recent years. In fact, most people are concerned that overall air quality is much worse than before, mainly due to increasing car ownership and use of chemicals as well as accelerating urbanization. For the most part, Korea's air quality standards are based on those recommended by the World Health Organization (WHO). The current standards are concerned with 26 pollutants, including sulfurous acid gas, carbon monoxide, nitrogen dioxide, smoke and particles, ozone, and lead. In selected industrial areas (Ulsan Mipo-Onsan and Yeocheon), more stringent or special standards are applied. To monitor air pollution, MOE and local governments operate automatic telemetering systems across the country. The government uses mobile monitoring vehicles to measure air pollu-

Table 3.1   Environmental Standards and Relevant Laws by Sector

Sector	Environmental Standards	Relevant Laws
Water Quality (rivers, lakes, underground water, marine areas)	Drinking water	Basic Environmental Policy Act
	Effluent water quality	Water Quality
	Wastewater discharge	Water Quality Preservation Act
		Act on Treatment of Sewage, Excreta, and Livestock Wastewater
Air Quality	Air emission	Air Quality Preservation Act
	Emission by manufactured motor vehicles	
	Emission by motor vehicles in operation	
Noise and Vibration	Manufacturing plant noise and vibration	Noise and Vibration Control Act
	Automobile noise	
Soil Preservation and Toxic Chemicals Management	Soil contamination	Soil Environment Preservation Act
	Restrictions on growing agricultural and fish products	Toxic Chemicals Control Act
	Designating toxic substances and other hazardous substances	

Source: "1999 Environment White Paper," MOE (October 1999).

tion in the areas where a telemetering system is not installed. It also maintains a rain acidity monitoring network in major urban areas. The violation rate based on total cases of inspection decreased from 9.2 percent in 1993 to 5.6 percent in 1997, but it increased to 7.4 percent in 1998. While the decrease is attributable to the government's more stringent enforcement efforts, it is also due to stagnant business activity because of the economic crisis.

Solid and Hazardous Waste Management

Since 1993, total waste volume has moved upward. In the 1990s, industrial waste discharges surged at an annual average of 10 percent while municipal waste discharges have been reduced significantly. Government waste management policy focuses more on expanding incineration capacity than increasing landfills, with a goal to raise the rate of incineration from 9 percent in 1998 to 20 percent in 2001. There were 12 incineration plants operating in 1997, and the government has pursued 20 new municipal incineration projects to be completed or started by 2001. The government places long-term policy priority on prevention or reduction, reuse, recycling, energy recovery, incineration, and landfill in that order. On the other hand, the government prohibits installing smaller incinerators with a processing capacity no larger than 25 kilograms per hour.

Chapter 4
Water and Wastewater

Institutional Structure

Korea's legal framework and government policy for the water and wastewater sub-sector saw great changes and advances in the 1990s. In 1990, the Water Quality Preservation Act spun off from the previous Environmental Preservation Act. In 1991, the Act on Treatment of Sewage, Excreta and Livestock Wastewater was separately enacted. In 1993, the Ministry of Environment established comprehensive measures for clean water supply for 1993-1997. At the same time, the government streamlined inter-agency complexities on environmental issues by rendering greater power to MOE to efficiently execute policy measures. Meanwhile, a series of water pollution accidents in major rivers evoked national concerns about safety with drinking water. To effectively solve these problems, MOE took over the authority and responsibility for water supply and wastewater management from the Ministry of Construction, and it undertook those for managing drinking water from the Ministry of Health and Social Affairs.

In 1996, MOE established comprehensive measures for water management for 1996 through 2005. Since then, MOE has implemented various measures to preserve the water environment and manage water resources. In 1998, the quality of Paldang Lake, the water resource for the Seoul Metropolitan area, including Inchon and Kyonggi-do, degraded to a serious level, and the press, NGOs, and other opinion leaders brought this issue to the public's attention. As a result, the Act on Improvement of Quality of Water Resources of the Han River was enacted in November 1998.

MOE is responsible for establishing national environmental policies and action plans for environmental protection and pollution control. Its Water Quality Management Bureau and the Water Supply and Sewage Treatment Bureau oversee water and wastewater matters. Each bureau consists of several divisions.

The Han River Watershed EMO, the Nakdong River EMO, the Youngsan River EMO, and the Keum River EMO manage environmental issues for the four major rivers that are the main water sources. With the exception of the Han River Watershed EMO, they are responsible for all environmental matters on a regional level, including water, wastewater, air, solid waste, and so forth, although local governments handle some practical functions, such as managing municipal wastewater. The Han River Watershed EMO is responsible for managing environmental issues involving the watershed only. Four local environmental management offices (LEMOs) and eight environmental branch offices operate under the environmental management offices.

Current water environment policy consists of five elements:

1. Pollution prevention
2. Pollution abatement and reduction
3. River environment management
4. Surveillance and inspection of discharging establishments
5. Monitoring and assessment

Table 4.1   Regional Environmental Management Offices (EMOs)

Han River Watershed EMO	Nakdong River EMO	Youngsan River EMO	Keum River EMO
Seoul Metro City	Pusan Metro City	Kwangju Metro City	Taejon Metro City
Inchon Metro City	Taegu Metro City	Chollanam-do	Chungchongnam-do
Kyonggi-do	Ulsan Metro City	Chollabuk-do	Chungchongbuk-do
Kangwon-do	Kyongsangnam-do	Cheju-do	
	Kyongsangbuk-do		

Source: MOE Web site, *www.me.gc.ka* (September 2000).

Table 4.2 Organizational Structure of Environmental Management Offices (EMOs)

Han River Watershed	Regional EMOs (Nakdong River, Youngsan River, Keum River)
Watershed Management Bureau	Operations Bureau
• Watershed Planning Division	• Operations Division
• Financial Planning Division	• Natural Environment Division
• Water Supply Source Management Division	• Compliance Monitoring Division
• Regional Cooperation Division	• Monitoring and Analysis Division
• Measurement and Analysis Division	• Administrative Management Division
• General Affairs Division	Environmental Branch Offices (8)
Han River Environmental Inspection Board	Local Environmental Management Offices (4)

Source: MOE Web site, *www.me.go.ka* (September 2000).

Table 4.3 Locations of Local Environmental Offices

Local environmental management offices (LEMOs)	Environmental Branch Offices
Kyong-In (Seoul and Inchon)	Kumi, Kyongsangbuk-do
Wonju, Kangwon-do	Pohang, Kyongsangbuk-do
Chonju, Chollabuk-do	Ulsan Metro City
Taegu Metro City	Chongju, Chungchungbuk-do
	Yeosu, Chollanam-do
	Cheju, Cheju-do
	Ansan, Kyonggi-do
	Chunchon, Kangwon-do

Source: MOE Web site, *www.me.go.ka* (September 2000).

Environmental Infrastructure

For the period 1993–1997, the government's total spending on water and wastewater infrastructure projects totaled approximately $21 billion, of which $9.7 billion was spent on wastewater treatment, sewerage, and other water quality improvement projects, and $11.1 billion on water supply and purification projects.

Under its long-term plan, which goes through 2005, MOE plans to invest approximately $25 billion on infrastructure projects for water quality improvement (see Table 4.5 for goals).

Water Supply

In Korea, water supply systems are classified into general (municipal), industrial, and private. The general or municipal water is further broken down into three categories: local, temporary, and regional. Local governments are responsible for supplying local municipal water and temporary water. The Ministry of Construction and Transportation is responsible for supplying regional mu-

nicipal water, but management of regional municipal water is commissioned to the state-run Korea Water Resource Management Corporation. Building and operating local municipal water and temporary water systems require approval from the Ministry of Environment and the relevant regional government.

Thus local governments manage all practical matters on the local level relating to the municipal water supply service, including planning water supply, maintaining and expanding water supply facilities, and determining fees. The national government establishes comprehensive plans and policy measures for water supply and supports local governments on technological and financing issues. The Korea Water Resource Management Corporation manages all practical matters involving regional water systems based on the national government's plans.

Until the mid-1990s, Korea's water supply policy focused on urban areas. In Korea's seven largest cities, around 98 percent of the population was served by the municipal water system in 1998, compared with 20.8 percent in agricultural areas and 88.6 percent in smaller cities. Over the next several years, the government plans

Table 4.4   Environmental Status of the Four Major Watershed Regions, 1999

Region	Han River	Nakdong River	Keum River	Youngsan River
Main watersheds	BukHan River NamHan River Ansung-cheon	Nakdong River Taehwa River Hyongsan River	Keum River Mankyong River Dongjin River Sapkyo-cheon	Youngsan River Seomjin River Tamjin River
Total length of watersheds (km)	481.7	521.5	395.5	136.0
Area (sq. km)	21,200	32,280	17,767	16,886
Annual average precipitation (mm)	1,286	1,137	1,268	1,400
Population (millions)	23.5	13.2	5.8	4.3
Livestock head (thousands)	940	3,600	4,270	2,820
Number of effluent facilities	17,999	12,058	6,089	3,793
Ratio of wastewater treatment of total effluent	76.4	56.3	31.4	43.8
Main water resources	Paldang Lake Chamsil Water Resource	Mulgeum Maeri Water Resource	Daechon Lake	Juam Lake

Source: Ministry of Environment, *1999 Environment White Paper* (October 1999).

Table 4.5   Major Goals of the Comprehensive Measures for Water Management, 1996–2005

Indicator	1996	2005	Remark
Ratio of municipal wastewater treatment (percent)	50	80	Based on population served by public treatment
Ratio of livestock wastewater treatment (percent)	42	74	Based on public treatment
Ratio of industrial wastewater treatment (percent)	73	90	Based on public treatment in industrial estates

Source: Ministry of Environment, *1999 Environment White Paper* (October 1999).

Table 4.6   Status of Environmental Infrastructure, 1998

Type		Total	Han River	Nak-dong River	Keum River	Youngsan River	Other
Wastewater treatment	No. plants	114	45	20	10	5	34
	Capacity*	16,618	8,097	2,917	995	700	3,909
Night soil treatment	No. plants	183	45	32	20	8	78
	Capacity*	28	11	4	2	1	12
Industrial waste-water treatment	No. plants	119	7	36	24	9	43
	Capacity*	702	7	330	114	5	246
Livestock wastewater	No. plants	10	5	2	1	—	2
	Capacity*	3	2	0.3	0.3	—	0.4
Total	**No. plants**	**426**	**102**	**90**	**55**	**22**	**157**
	Capacity*	**17,351**	**8,116**	**3,251**	**1,111**	**706**	**4,167**

*Capacity in thousand of tons per day.

Source: Ministry of Environment, *1999 Environment White Paper* (October 1999).

Table 4.7 Investments in Environmental Infrastructure Projects, 1998

Type	Value (in billions of won)	Number of Projects, etc.	Capacity (in thousands of tons)
Municipal wastewater treatment	1,322.8	21	1,578.6
Sewerage maintenance	915.0	(4,121*)	n.a.
Night soil treatment	44.0	7	1.2
Industrial wastewater treatment	85.9	1	1.0
Livestock wastewater treatment	41.4	3	.5
Cleaning of polluted rivers	45.5	(23**)	n.a
Total	**2,454.6**	**32**	**1,581.3**

*total length in kilometers

**number of rivers

n.a. – not applicable

Note: Average exchange rate in 1998: US$1 – Korean won, 399

Source: Ministry of Environment, *1999 Environment White Paper* (October 1999).

Table 4.8 Water Supply Development Plan for Agricultural Areas

	1995– 1998	1999	2000– 2004	Total 1995– 2004
Number of projects	78	12	125	215
Value of investment (billions of won)	224	87	489	746
Value of investment (millions of U.S. dollars)	228	73	445	770

Source: Ministry of Environment, *1999 Environment White Paper* (October 1999).

Table 4.9 Water Supply Development Plan for Medium and Small Cities

	1995– 1998	1999	2000– 2004	Total 1995– 2004
Number of projects	50	8	23	81
Value of investment (billions of won)	243	144	530	917
Value of investment (millions of U.S. dollars)	247	121	482	850

Source: Ministry of Environment, *1999 Environment White Paper* (October 1999).

Table 4.10 Water Supply Development Plan for Islands

	1995– 1998	1999	2000– 2002	Total 1995– 2004
Number of projects	36	8	21	65
Value of investment (billions of won)	38	22	92	152
Value of investment (millions of U.S. dollars)	39	18	84	141

Source: Ministry of Environment, *1999 Environment White Paper* (October 1999).

to expand water supply capacity for these less developed areas. (See Tables 4.8, 4.9, and 4.10.)

As the quality of water sources deteriorated significantly, the Korean government decided to adopt advanced purification technology and equipment at 17 purification plants between 1996 and 2002. By 1999, 10 such projects were completed and the remaining seven projects will be completed by 2002. The total budget for the 17 projects is $364 million. In addition, the government plans to spend a total of $2.8 billion between 2000 and 2011 to improve existing water supply facilities such as water pipelines, reservoirs, and purification plants.

Drinking Water

Korea's current standard for municipal drinking water quality involves 45 different chemicals. Based on the World Health Organization's recommendation and the U.S. standard, MOE has checked 301 chemicals at major purification plants nationwide since 1989 and continues to adopt higher standards to ensure high-quality municipal drinking water.

Regional governments began regulating bottled drinking water in 1995. Currently, 51 chemicals are subject to the standards for bottled drinking water. In 1999, 73 licensed manufacturers provided bottled water, with total 1998 sales of 940,356 tons or $82 million. There are more than 3 million purifiers installed in homes since many consumers do not trust the quality of drinking tap water. The government began to regulate manufacturing, importation, and sales of purifiers in 1997. The annual market size of home purifiers for 1998 was estimated at 260,000 units (including 30,000 imported units) or $188 million, including $21 million from imports. The estimated market size for 1999 is $250 million.

Municipal Wastewater

Local governments are responsible for building and operating public sewage systems, while the Ministry of Environment has the authority to approve municipal wastewater treatment projects in consultation with the Ministry of Construction and Transportation. Some local governments also use their own companies to operate municipal sewage systems. Regional governments are responsible for issuing approval for sewerage pipeline projects.

The volume of municipal wastewater effluent has increased recently and now exceeds 16.3 million cubic meters a day. The Korean government began to increase investments in municipal wastewater treatment facilities in the early 1990s as part of its efforts to ensure a clean water supply for 1993–1997. As a result, there were 114 public sewage treatment plants operating nationwide in 1998, which treated 65.9 percent of the total municipal wastewater, up from only 38.8 percent in 1992.

In 1999, the Korean government invested approximately $1 billion for 44 sewage treatment projects (36 new projects and 8 expansion projects) for a total daily capacity of 1 million cubic meters. The government plans to raise the public treatment rate to 80 percent in 2005

under the current long-term water quality management plan. To that end, the government is building 165 new sewage treatment plants to increase the nation's capacity by 12.7 million cubic meters per day by 2005.

Industrial Wastewater

Since the Water Quality Preservation Act was enacted in 1990 to effectively manage industrial wastewater, the Korean government has amended this act seven times to cope with changing environmental conditions and needs.

The government manages industrial wastewater mainly through the following methods:

- Regulations of construction permits for wastewater discharging facilities
- Legal standards for industrial effluents
- Guidance and inspection to make sure that polluters conform to the standards
- Imposing discharge fees
- Construction and operation of industrial waste treatment facilities in major industrial estates

Between 1983 and 1991, the national government built six public industrial wastewater treatment plants in major national industrial estates. Since then, the government has adopted a "polluters pay" principle that requires polluters to build pollution treatment facilities with their own funds. In 1997, the government began providing a subsidy of 50 percent of the total needed funding required for each project in selected industrial estates.

Nationwide, 39 industrial wastewater treatment plants represent a total daily capacity of 728,000 tons (based on 1998 data), or approximately 80 percent of total industrial wastewater discharge. The government plans to have a total of 53 industrial wastewater treatment plants (i.e., 14 new plants) operating to raise the percentage of public treatment to 90 percent by 2005.

Table 4.11 Trends in Public Sewage Treatment, 1992–1998

	1992	1994	1996	1997	1998
a = Population (in thousands)	44,569	45,512	46,426	46,878	47,174
b = Population treated (in thousands)	17,279	19,081	24,420	28,559	31,099
Percentage of treatment (b/a)	38.8	41.9	52.6	60.9	65.9
Number of plants	26	57	79	93	114
Total capacity (thousand of tons per day)	**5,815**	**9,391**	**11,452**	**15,038**	**16,616**

Source: Ministry of Environment, *1999 Environment White Paper* (October 1999).

Table 4.12 Status of Industrial Wastewater Discharge by Watershed Region, 1998

	Han River	Nak-dong River	Keum River	Young-san River	Coastal Areas	Other	Total
Number of businesses	10,558	5,690	3,137	1,381	11,206	5,649	37,621
Volume of discharge (m³ per day)	384,416	490,620	195,923	53,574	1,140,342	349,305	2,614,180
Biological oxygen demand generated (kg per day)	380,227	511,914	282,741	84,786	971,145	398,264	2,629,077
Biological oxygen demand discharged (kg per day)	13,042	23,070	7,707	2,105	36,167	15,166	97,257

Source: Ministry of Environment, *1999 Environment White Paper* (October 1999).

Table 4.13 Number of Industrial Wastewater Discharging Establishments

Year	Class 1 (2,000 m³ or more per day)	Class 2 (700 to less than 2,000 m³ per day)	Class 3 (200 to less than 700 m³ per day)	Class 4 (50 to less than 200 m³ per day)	Class 5 (Less than 50 m³ per day)	Total
1995	27,754	272	391	681	2,452	25,681
1996	28,102	279	428	869	2,223	24,213
1997	39,939	275	427	986	2,002	36,249
1998	37,621	241	433	1,034	2,036	33,877

Source: Environmental Management Research Center, *2000 Environmental Industry Yearbook* (Seoul, 1999).

The Ministry of Environment surveys businesses discharging industrial wastewater each year and maintains a database. These surveys indicate that the number of discharging businesses grew to 39,939 in 1997 but declined to 37,621 in 1998 during the economic crisis. Discharging businesses are categorized into five classes based on the volume of wastewater discharge. Major polluting industries are transportation equipment, metal, food and beverage, textile, leather, and paper.

Market Size, Competitive Situation, and Market Opportunities

Korea's market for the water and wastewater sub-sector was estimated at $3.3 billion in 1999, representing 46 percent of the total environmental market valued at $7.1 billion. In the same year, the government spent $2.2 billion for managing water quality and wastewater, and industry spent $0.9 billion for pollution control in the water and wastewater sub-sector.

Over the last several years, the government's investment in water and wastewater infrastructure increased from around $1.2 billion in 1995 to approximately $2 billion in 1997. In 1998, investment declined to $1.6 billion during the economic crisis but rose by 6.8 percent to $1.7 billion in 1999.

Industry investment in wastewater treatment projects peaked at $498 million in 1996, declined to $363 million in 1997, and declined again to $236 million in 1998. While investment declined further in 1999 to $216 million, operational spending on environmental facilities increased by 9.8 percent from $553 million in 1998 to $607 million in 1999 as business activity expanded.

MOE plans to invest a total of $230 million in developing environmental infrastructure for wastewater treatment between 2000 and 2005, consisting of $214 million for sewage treatment plants and $16 million for livestock wastewater treatment facilities. The budget for water quality and wastewater management allocated to the Ministry of Environment for 2000 is $364 million, up by 15 percent from $323 million in 1999.

According to the Korea Environmental Industry Association, in 1998 Korea's pollution control industry conducted 1,427 water pollution control projects, both public and private, valued at $718 million. There are 775 companies that are licensed as pollution control contractors. Of these licensed contractors, 574 firms are qualified for the water/wastewater field. Major contractors typically hold licenses for all of the pollution control fields: air,

Table 4.14   Upcoming Public Sewage Treatment Projects, 2000–2005

	2000	2001	2002	2003	2004	2005
Capacity	1,834	861	1,564	886	1,827	5,833
(in thousands of tons per day)	36	30	33	18	18	65
Number of plants (projects)	1,497	1,464	1,540	1,625	1,722	1,975
Planned investment (billions of won)	1,361	1,331	1,400	1,447	1,565	1,795
Planned investment* (billions of U.S. dollars)	1.24	1.21	1.27	1.31	1.42	1.63

*Average exchange rate projection for 2000 through 2005: US$1 — 1,100 won.

Source: Environmental Management Research Center, *2000 Environmental Industry Yearbook* (Seoul, 1999).

water, and noise/vibration. There are 47 such general environmental contractors, many of which are divisions of major engineering and construction companies. Major players in the pollution control field are engineering and construction companies affiliated with Korean conglomerates, such as Samsung, Hyundai, LG, Lotte, Ssangyong, Keumho, Doosan, and Dongbu, and several leading independent construction firms, such as Dong-Ah, Namkwang, and Limkwang. (See Appendices E and F for more company information.)

Foreign firms also participate in pollution control projects, usually as suppliers or subcontractors to Korean firms. They provide technology and/or equipment for specific areas, such as purification and sludge treatment, where Korean companies lack technological capability. Korea's environmental technology has advanced largely through licensing from foreign firms. By 1996, there were 76 cases of license agreement reported in the water pollution control field. (Note: Statistics for licensing are not available for the years after 1996 when licensing arrangements were deregulated.) In the past, the market for foreign pollution control technologies, including water pollution control, was dominated by Japanese firms with an estimated share of 50 to 60 percent, followed by U.S. companies representing 20 to 25 percent. The remaining 20 percent or so originated from European firms.

U.S. environmental companies that have been active in Korea as technology and equipment suppliers in the field of water and wastewater include CH2M Hill (water treatment), Romm & Hasy (filtering machines), Hydranautics (membrane products), Filterk Corp. (backwashable micro filter products), VMT (pure water treatment), and Aeromix Systems (surface aerator). Japanese and European suppliers include Led Italia (Italy), Danish Hydraulic Institute (Denmark), Daiki (Japan), Rochem (Germany), TIA (France), Daiwa (Japan), NCE (Japan), Biothane System (Netherlands), Toyobo (Japan), Denka Engineering (Japan), Trailigas (France), Nitto

Denko (Japan), Suirei (Japan), Nittetsu Chemical Engineering (Japan), and YIT (Finland).

Joint Ventures and Licensing

Recently, several foreign firms have entered the environmental infrastructure market by establishing partnerships with major Korean contractors. In January 2000, the Construction Division of Samsung Corporation announced that the company signed a joint venture agreement with Operation Management International, Inc. (OMI), a subsidiary of CH2M Hill that is a U.S.-based multinational engineering company, in order to pursue sewage treatment projects. According to Samsung, OMI will not only provide financing but will also transfer advanced technologies for sewage treatment. LG Engineering & Construction has recently introduced technologies from several Japanese and U.S. companies in the fields of sewage treatment and solid waste incineration. Hyundai Engineering & Construction is pursuing a joint venture with Generale Desaux of France, which specializes in water and wastewater treatment, for an infrastructure project in Kyongsangbuk-do.

Privatization

The Korean government decided to introduce private funds for local sewage treatment projects in areas where the local government is not able to secure funding. The Ministry of Environment has selected 16 sewage treatment projects for privatization. Whether a sewage treatment project is privatized is determined by an agreement among MOE, the local government, and the state-run Korea Environmental Management Corporation (KEMC). KEMC provides technical and operational supports to local governments in managing environmental infrastructures. As evidenced by OMI's partnership with Samsung, privatization offers good opportunities for U.S. companies to enter or grow in the Korean environmental infrastructure market.

Chapter 5
Solid Waste

This chapter covers municipal and industrial solid waste management and disposal, including landfill, incineration, waste-to-energy, and recycling.

Institutional Structure

Korea's legal system for managing solid waste is based on the Waste Management Act of 1992. Other acts related to this sector are the Act on Promotion of Resources Saving and Reutilization, the Act on Promotion of Waste Treatment Facilities and Surrounding Communities, and the Act on Trans-boundary Movement and Disposal of Waste.

Local governments are responsible for the collection, transport, and treatment of municipal waste while discharging businesses must treat their own waste, whether it is industrial, construction, or hazardous waste. The national government establishes basic policies and supports local governments on technological and financial issues, while provincial governments coordinate with the national and local governments and provide financial support to them.

The Waste Management and Recycling Bureau, a part of the Ministry of Environment, administers this sub-sector and includes five divisions:

- Waste Management Policy
- Municipal Waste Management
- Industrial Waste Management
- Resource Recycling
- Chemicals Management

In Korea, total solid waste volume gradually increased from 141,400 tons per day in 1993 to 194,700 tons per day in 1997. Korea's total municipal waste volume has been on a downward trend since 1990, but industrial waste (consisting of "general" and "specified" waste) has increased at an annual average rate of more than 10 percent, surpassing the volume of municipal waste in 1993. Korea's per-capita municipal waste volume declined from 1.3 kilograms in 1994 to 0.96 kilograms in 1998 as a result of the enforcement of a 1995 government regulation.

Korea's waste management policy prioritizes management approaches in the following order: reduction, reuse, recycling, energy recovery, incineration, and landfill. Reduction, reuse, recycling, and energy recovery are collectively called "waste minimization." In 1993, MOE established the Comprehensive Plan for National Waste Treatment for 1993-2001. In 1996, this long-term plan was revised into the Comprehensive Plan for National Waste Management for the remaining period to reflect changes in relevant regulations.

In Korea, the majority of municipal wastes are still treated by landfill. The proportion of recycled waste to all industrial waste is relatively high, but the volume of industrial waste treated by landfill is similar to that of municipal waste. The goals of the Comprehensive Plan are based on the following principles:

- Encourage recycling and discourage landfill.
- Prevent or reduce waste generation and expand recycling capacity.
- Expand incineration capacity for the waste that cannot be recycled.

Table 5.1   Goals of Waste Management, 1995–2001

	Municipal Waste			Industrial Waste		
	1995	1998	2001	1995	1998	2001
Incineration	4.0	15.0	20.0	6.3	10.0	12.0
Landfill	72.3	55.0	45.0	32.5	25.0	20.0
Recycling	23.7	30.0	35.0	61.2	65.0	68.0

Note: Figures shown are percentages of total disposal.

Source: Ministry of Environment, *1999 Environment White Paper* (October 1999).

Table 5.2 MOE Long-term Objectives of Recycling by Industry

	1997	*1998–2001*	*2002–2004*
Paper	50	55	60
Glass (glass containers)	47	52	60 (45)
Steel cans	30	40	52
Plastics:			
PET containers	25	45	55
Other plastics	10	20	25
Other products made of plastics	—	5	10

Note: Figures are percentages of total waste generated.

Source: Ministry of Environment, *1999 Environment White Paper* (October 1999).

In order to support the underdeveloped recycling industry, beween 1994 and 1999, the government provided $180 million in low-interest loans to 12 private firms. In 2000, $45 million is allocated to support three new plants and three ongoing projects in the private sector. In addition to private recycling plants, the state-run Korea Resources Recovery and Reutilization Corporation (KORECO) operates 25 recycling plants for plastics, tires, and glass bottles. The government regulates the recycling of specified waste including iron and steel slag, coal products, and three types of construction material.

Environmental Infrastructure

Since 1993, the Korean government has continued to expand investment in incineration facilities, public landfills, and food waste treatment facilities. In addition, MOE has supported local governments in building integrated waste treatment facilities in agricultural areas and maintaining used landfills. In 2000, MOE allocated $134 million to support these projects.

Municipal incineration: Under the Korean government's strong drive to expand incineration capacity for municipal waste, local governments built 44 incineration plants, including 17 large-scale plants,[1] between 1993 and 1999 with subsidies from national and regional governments. The total value of the 17 large incineration projects currently operating is $592 million. In 2000, 23 new municipal incineration projects and 24 expansion projects are being started nationwide,[2] for which MOE grants a $60 million subsidy. From 2001 through 2005, local governments will start 21 new incineration projects and 41 expansion projects nationwide. Over this period, MOE plans to provide a total subsidy of $140 million to regional governments for 27 expansion projects at the existing incineration plant sites.

Municipal landfill: In 1998, 442 municipal landfills nationwide encompassed a total land area of 29.6 million square meters and a total capacity of 408.9 million cubic meters (or the remaining capacity of 312,393,000 cubic meters). Between 1993 and 1999, 26 landfill projects (7 million square meters) were completed and operating, and 27 landfill sites (3.3 million square meters) were under construction as of the end of 1999. In 2000, eight additional landfill projects are being started. For 2001 through 2004, the government plans to invest $389 million in building a new landfill site and expanding or upgrading 13 existing landfills.

Agricultural waste treatment plants: The federal government plans to build integrated waste treatment plants designed to systematically integrate incineration, recycling, and landfill for agricultural areas where municipal waste treatment systems are less developed. Between 1993 and 1999, 65 such integrated waste treatment plants were constructed in agricultural areas, and 10 new projects are being started in 2000. For 2001 through 2004, the government plans to start three new projects and 78

---

1. Locations of the 17 large municipal incineration plants operating as of June 30, 2000 are: Seoul Nowon, Seoul Yangchon, Pusan Dadae, Pusan Haewoondae, Taegu Songso, Taejon Taedok 1, Ulsan, Anyang Pyongchon (Kyonggi-do), Koyang Ilsan (Kyonggi-do), Puchon Chungdong (Kyonggi-do), Songnam (Kyonggi-do), Kwangmyong (Kyonggi-do), Yongin (Kyonggi-do), Yongin Suji (Kyonggi-do), Suwon (Kyonggi-do), Kwachon (Kyonggi-do), and Changwon 1 (Kyongsangnam-do).

2. As of June 30, 2000, 16 municipal incineration projects were in progress in these areas: Seoul Kangnam, Pusan Myongji, Taejon Taedok 2, Inchon Kyongso, Kwangju Sangmu, Kunpo Sanbon (Kyonggi-do), Puchon Daejang (Kyonggi-do), Ansan (Kyonggi-do), Kuri (Kyonggi-do), Euijongbu (Kyonggi-do), Paju (Kyonggi-do), Changwon 2 (Kyongsangnam-do), Kimhae Jangyu (Kyongsangnam-do), Chonan (Chungchongnam-do), Cheju Sanbuk, and Cheju Sannam. The total value of these 16 ongoing incineration projects is $707 million.

expansion projects with a total investment of $166 million within the existing facilities in agricultural areas.

Market Size, Competitive Situation, and Market Opportunities

Based on the Bank of Korea's environmental expenditure data released in October 2000 for 1999, the Korean market for all solid waste treatment products and services was estimated to be $2.5 billion, consisting of $1.6 billion for the public sector and $0.5 billion for the private sector. Over the last several years, government investment in solid waste treatment facilities progressively increased: from $323 million in 1995 to approximately $500 million in 1999. In the private sector, facility investment in waste treatment peaked at $314 million in 1996. The size of the private sector market declined to $234 million in 1997 and further to $165 million in 1998 during the economic crisis. In 1999, the private-sector market for solid waste treatment facilities grew 4.8 percent over the previous year to reach $173 million.

Since 1993, Korea's municipal incineration infrastructure market has offered lucrative opportunities for foreign firms that have advanced technology and/or equipment. U.S. firms seem to have largely neglected or lost these opportunities in this fast-growing market segment, while Japanese, German, and other European engineering and equipment firms have entered and built their positions in the market by taking part in major projects under licensing agreements with Korean partners.

In the market for municipal incineration, major Korean engineering and construction companies typically act as prime contractors for large municipal incineration projects. The majority of these contractors are subsidiaries of conglomerates, such as Hyundai, Samsung, LG, SK, Kolon, Dongbu, and Daewoo. Foreign engineering firms and equipment manufacturers typically take part in these projects as sub-contractors or technology/equipment suppliers. As shown in the table above, no U.S. engineering firm has participated in Korea's major municipal incineration projects.

Korean equipment manufacturers are now capable of making medium- to low-tech components and parts with acceptable quality. But they still lack core technologies, such as the heat treatment technology for fabricating the furnace stall part of an incinerator and the incineration ash treatment technology to abate hazardous matters such as heavy metals. Since the municipal incineration market emerged in the 1980s, Japanese suppliers have built strong positions based on their proximity in terms of geographic, practical, and cultural aspects as well as on their low-cost advantage. The Japanese environmental industry has advanced largely by acquiring European, mainly German, technology through licensing. Generally, German and other European companies have enjoyed quality images in the Korean industry and government.

As in advanced nations, the stroker type of incineration technology with a whirl reactor has become the industry standard for municipal incineration in Korea since the early 1990s. In the past, municipal incinerators typically had a daily processing capacity of 100 to 200 tons. In recent years, several larger incinerators with a capacity of over 400 tons per day have been installed.

The solid waste recycling segment of the market is still largely less developed compared to U.S., European,

Table 5.3   Foreign Companies Active in Korea's Market for Municipal Incinerators

Country	Foreign Company	Korean Partner
Japan	Hitachi Zosen	Daewoo Corp.
	Kawasaki Heavy Industry	LG Construction
	Mitsubishi Heavy Industry	Samsung Heavy Industry
	Sanki	Kolon Engineering & Construction
	NKK	Jindo Construction
Germany	Deutsche Babcock	Hyundai Heavy Industry
	Steinmuller	Dongbu Corp.
Denmark	Volund	Halla Industry Development
Belgium	Seghers	SK Engineering & Construction
France	Stein Industry	Samsung Corp.
Switzerland	ABB	SK Engineering & Construction
		Hyundai Precision & Industry

Source: Adapted from: Ministry of Environment, *Status of Municipal Incinerators* (June 2000).

or Japanese standards. Five large-scale recycling plants nationwide (one operated by the state-run KORECO, and four privately owned and operated) shred, sort and separate steel, other metals, plastics, other combustible and non-combustible wastes. According to industry sources, domestic producers supply the great majority of recycling equipment used in the Korean industry.

For U.S. environmental companies, opportunities can be found mainly with plasma technology that can be applied to both municipal and commercial incinerators in various sizes. Another area of opportunity associated with incineration is that of controlling dioxin emissions and other toxic substances such as volatile organic compounds (VOCs). MOE has drafted standards for dioxin emission for smaller, unregulated incinerators. At the same time, the government has prohibited building small incineration facilities with an hourly capacity of no larger than 25 kilograms.

Future opportunities will also emerge in Korea's less developed recycling and energy recovery and waste-to-energy fields. Although the Korean government has placed a higher priority on these fields than incineration or landfill in establishing the long-term policy goals, they still lack infrastructure, technology, and regulation. For instance, many local governments now collect more recyclable waste than can be stored, but they do not have proper systems to recycle them. The government plans to expand the proportion of recycling industrial waste to 75 percent by 2005 from its current level of approximately 67 percent. The government has also reviewed a model project of the so-called Eco-Industrial Complex oriented toward the zero discharge of solid waste. At the same time, Korean industries will increasingly need advanced technologies to reuse or recycle industrial waste, scrapped cars, computers, and home appliances in order to meet the growing demand for global environmental protection from advanced economies.

In Korea, the waste-to-energy market is just now emerging, because Korean firms lack technological capability and experience. In October 2000, MOE invited bids for a waste-to-energy project involving the reuse of landfill gas in power generation using steam turbines at the Inchon landfill site. The budget allocated for this project is $62 million. Meanwhile, the government has introduced new regulations to reduce food waste. As part of these efforts, it has encouraged industry to build private facilities for the reuse of food waste into animal feed or fertilizer by granting government subsidies while continuing to build new public facilities. The government plans to continue its efforts to raise the percentage of food waste reuse to 50 percent by 2002 from 34.4 percent in 1999.

Chapter 6
Hazardous Waste

This chapter covers hazardous waste management and remediation of medical waste, hydrocarbons, heavy metals, and other hazardous industrial wastes.

Institutional Structure

Under the current legal system for environmental management in Korea, hazardous wastes correspond to "specified" wastes, which fall under the industrial waste category. The Waste Management Act regulates hazardous industrial waste, general industrial waste, and construction waste. Currently, approximately 11,000 companies are designated as hazardous waste generators, and 20 types of waste are regulated as "specified" or hazardous wastes, including sludge, industrial dust, organic solvents, acid wastes, alkaline wastes, oil wastes, paint and plastic wastes. In 1998, 53.6 percent of total hazardous waste was recycled, 28.4 percent was incinerated, and 8.8 percent was disposed in landfills.

Each discharging business is required to dispose of its own industrial waste, including specified wastes. The number and ratio of violations decreased from 812 cases (15.7 percent of total inspections) in 1995 to 354 cases (6.1 percent of total inspections) in 1998. In 1999, the Waste Management Act was amended to require discharging businesses to register the paths of hazardous waste treatment and to stiffen the penalty imposed on violations. Currently, 494 toxic chemicals are regulated by the Toxic Chemicals Control Act. Among these toxic chemicals, 22 chemicals are classified as "restricted" and 29 as "prohibited." Toxic chemicals manufacturers located in designated industrial estates should be registered with their regional environmental management offices under MOE, and other producers should be registered with their provincial governments. In 1998, there were 325 registered toxic chemicals manufacturers, 1,522 distributors, and 2,018 dealers. The manufacturing, importing, and/or selling of toxic chemicals are regulated by the Toxic Chemicals Control Act, and the discharging of pollutants and wastes is regulated by the Air Quality Preservation Act, the Water Quality Preservation Act, and the Waste Management Act. Medical waste was loosely regulated by the Medical Act until August 9, 2000, when a new regulation became effective under the Waste Management Act. This new regulation provides stringent standards for collecting, transporting, storing, and disposing medical wastes to a level comparable to major advanced nations.

As discussed previously, Korea's hazardous waste management policy is planned and executed as a part of its industrial waste management. In line with the extended producer responsibility principle adopted by major European countries, the Korean government places more responsibility on producers than consumers in managing all types of solid waste including hazardous waste.

In order to reduce industrial waste, particularly hazardous waste, MOE and the Ministry of Commerce, Industry, and Energy (MOCIE) have jointly enforced the Regulation for Reduction of Industrial Waste since 1996, which requires private industries to reduce waste generation through such methods as process improvement and recycling. This regulation applies to 14 industries, including chemicals, electronics, materials, and transportation equipment, and over 600 manufacturing establishments nationwide that fall into these industries.

These selected manufacturing establishments account for only 1 percent of total manufacturing establishments designated as hazardous (specified) waste discharging businesses but represent as much as 86 percent of the total volume of hazardous waste discharges. Each selected company is responsible for establishing and managing the reduction plan. Various incentives are granted to those who are selected as "excellent manufacturing establishments." Currently, seven companies have been designated as "excellent," including three Samsung plants, SK Chemical Suwon Fabric Plant, and LG Chemical Chongju Plant.

Infrastructure Development

Hazardous waste discharging businesses can either have their own treatment facilities or commission disposal activities to contractors. In-house treatment represents around 25 percent of the total hazardous waste volume of 2.2 million tons per year, and the remaining 75 percent is disposed by hazardous waste treatment contractors. Treating specified industrial wastes is broadly

Table 6.1 Public Specified (Hazardous) Waste Treatment Infrastructure, 1998

Name	Location	Land area (000 m²)	Capacity (m³) Total capacity	Filled volume	Remaining capacity	Planned expansion (1999–2004)
Onsan Landfill	Ulsan Metro City	77	401,300	289,580	111,720	—
Kunsan Landfill	Kunsan, Chollabuk-do	66	73,400	33,150	40,250	366,950
Kunsan Incineration Plant	Kunsan, Chollabuk-do	(a)	60 tons per day	—	—	—
Kwangyang Landfill	Kwangyang, Chollanam-do	110	106,321	3831	102,490	749,171
Changwon Landfill	Changwon, Kyongsangnam-do	121	61,135	—	61,135	1,079,153
Total		**374**	**642,156**	**326,561**	**315,595**	**2,195,274**

m²: square meters; m³: cubic meters

(a) Korea Environmental Management Corporation operates both a landfill and an incineration plant within its Kunsan site.

Source: Environmental Management Research Center, *2000 Environmental Industry Yearbook* (Seoul, 1999).

classified into two categories: a) intermediate treatment and b) final treatment such as public landfill and public incineration. Currently, 45 private companies conduct the intermediate treatment of specified industrial waste, such as incineration, physical-chemical treatment, and solidification. The combined daily capacity of these firms is 6,846 tons per day.

There are five public hazardous waste treatment facilities located around four major industrial complexes, and three expansion or upgrade projects are planned for 2000 through 2004. Between 1993 and 1999, approximately $183 million was invested in expanding hazardous waste facilities.

Market Situation and Opportunities

Separate statistics are not available to determine the accurate size of the hazardous solid waste treatment market as this category is incorporated into the broader industrial waste category. In recent years, the size of the market for industrial waste treatment plants and equipment ranges from $104 million for 1998 to $430 million for 1996.

Growth potential for hazardous waste treatment technology and equipment is enormous as Korea's regulatory requirements for this sub-sector grow increasingly stringent and the environmental authorities adopt a more stringent stance in executing inspection of disposal activities and imposing penalties. In addition, the Korean government amended and began to enforce the Toxic

Chemicals Control Act in 1999 to conform to international environmental treaties and resolutions to effectively manage hazardous materials on a global basis. For instance, MOE plans to build a database by surveying all manufacturers, importers, and users of toxic chemicals. The data will be used to manage these substances effectively.

In addition, Korea pledged to introduce the Toxics Release Inventory (TRI) program when the nation joined the Organization for Economic Cooperation and Development (OECD) in 1997. In 1999, the petrochemical and

Table 6.2 Number of Hazardous Waste Discharging Establishments by Jurisdiction, 1998

Regional Agency	Number of Discharging Establishments
Han River EMO	4,123
Nakdong River EMO	1,265
Keum River EMO	759
Youngsan River EMO	707
Wonju LEMO	745
Taegu LEMO	2,257
Chonju LEMO	299
Inchon LEMO	731
Total	**10,886**

EMO: Environmental Management Office

LEMO: Local Environmental Management Office

Source: Environmental Management Research Center, *2000 Environmental Industry Yearbook* (Seoul, 1999).

Table 6.3   Number of Hazardous Waste Disposal Companies by Type of Service, 1998

Regional Agency	Collection and Transport	Intermediate Treatment	Final Treatment (Incineration)	Total
Total	83	45	6	134
Han River EMO	15	14	-	29
Nakdong River EMO	22	12	3	37
Keum River EMO	10	2	1	13
Youngsan River EMO	7	3	1	11
Taegu LEMO	8	3	1	12
Wonju LEMO	3	-	-	3
Inchon LEMO	13	9	-	22
Chonju LEMO	5	2	-	7
Total	**83**	**45**	**6**	**134**

EMO: Environmental Management Office

LEMO: Local Environmental Management Office

Source: Environmental Management Research Center, *2000 Environmental Industry Yearbook* (Seoul, 1999).

oil refining industries began to adopt TRI and the government plans to expand this program into other industries. The government is also conducting an extensive survey on environmental hormones to prepare proper regulations and enforcement measures. All these regulatory and administrative changes offer opportunities for international environmental companies specializing in hazardous waste management.

The main categories of hazardous waste discharged by Korean industries include acid waste (638,634 tons in 1998), alkaline waste (427,087 tons), non-halogen solvent waste (339,666 tons), dust powder (271,888 tons), oil waste (256,569 tons), and wastewater sludge (102,082 tons). According to industry sources, Korea particularly needs hazardous waste treatment technology in the following fields: dust treatment using the plasma incineration technology, recovery of oil-spilled soils and landfills, extrusion of incinerated waste using plasma for large-scale municipal waste incinerators.

Table 6.4   Hazardous Waste Volume by Treatment Method, 1998

Treatment Method	Discharged Volume (in tons per year)
In-house treatment	546,803
Contracted treatment:	
Recovery	900,248
Intermediate	322,407
Final treatment	98,964
Marine dumping	232,741
Public (landfill, incineration)	101,517
Carry-over	36,917
Accumulated storage	51,451
Total	**2,217,215**

Source: Environmental Management Research Center, *2000 Environmental Industry Yearbook* (Seoul, 1999).

Chapter 7
Air Pollution

This chapter covers industrial air pollution (including contributing to global warming and causing acid rain and human disease), vehicle emissions, and energy efficiency, including renewable energy technologies.

Institutional Structure

Korea's regulatory framework for managing air pollution control issues is based on the Air Quality Preservation Act of 1990 (amended in 1999). MOE is responsible for managing all environmental issues including air quality control on the national level, including policy planning and implementation.

MOE's Air Quality Management Bureau consists of four divisions:

1. Air Quality Policy
2. Air Pollution Control
3. Automotive Pollution Control
4. Noise, Vibration, and Dust Control

Air pollutants are defined as smoke, gases, and offensive odor having adverse impacts on human health and ecosystems. By law, 52 matters are currently defined as air pollutants. Air pollutants are broadly classified into gaseous matters and particulate matters. Gaseous matters are generated from the combustion of fuels or chemical reactions, such as nitrogen oxide, sulfur dioxide, carbon monoxide, and stratospheric ozone. Suspended particulate matters are defined as microscopic matters that are emitted from factories and other business establishments as a result of the combustion of fossil fuels or other processes.

The government began to establish standards for air pollution control in 1979. The standards became more stringent in 1995 and even more so in 1999. Based on the relevant provisions of the Air Quality Preservation Act, the more demanding standards are applied in Ulsan Mipo-Onsan and Yochon, two industrial areas.

Air pollution control standards are concerned with 26 substances, including sulfur dioxide (SO_2), carbon monoxide (CO), nitrogen dioxide (NO_2), total suspended particulates (TSP), particulate matters (PM-10), ozone (O_3), and lead (Pb). Since 1990, Korea's air quality has generally improved or remained relatively stable in terms of these major pollutants, except for ozone. In Seoul, for instance, the average annual ozone emission increased from 0.009 parts per meter in 1990 to 0.017 parts per meter in 1998 as a result of an increasing number of motor vehicles and more use of organic solvents. Other large cities in Korea such as Pusan, Taegu, Taejon, Kwangju, and Inchon show similar trends in terms of ozone emission.

More than 31,000 business establishments are listed with MOE as air pollutant emitting businesses. The regulatory authority on air pollution control over these emitting businesses is divided into regional governments and environmental management offices under the jurisdiction of MOE. Regional governments are responsible for managing more than 24,000 businesses, and MOE for approximately 7,000. Air pollutant emitting establishments are categorized into five classes depending on the volume of annual fuel consumption.

Regional governments and environmental offices conduct regular or surprise inspections of pollution emitting facilities. In 1998, they conducted a total of 48,149 inspections and found 2,286 violators (7.4 percent of total inspections), and 956 companies were subject to administrative orders or criminal indictment. The number and ratio of violation has decreased since 1993 as Korean companies have increased investments in air pollution control equipment.

To effectively accomplish this complex inspection program, the national government and local governments maintain monitoring systems, including telemetering systems, monitoring vehicles, and acid rain monitoring stations. Installing smokestack telemetering systems also is required or encouraged for certain emitters or in special industrial areas. In addition, the government has designated the Ulsan Mipo-Onsan National Industrial Complex and Yochon National Industrial Complex as special management areas. The environmental authorities also enforce specific measures for managing main air pollutants including sulfur dioxide, spreading particulate, of-

Table 7.1 Air Quality Standards

Pollutant	Standards	Measuring Method
Sulfur dioxide (SO^2)	Annual average 0.03 ppm 24-hour average 0.14 ppm Hourly average 0.25 ppm	Pulse U.V. fluorescence
Carbon monoxide (CO)	8-hour average 9 ppm Hourly average 25 ppm	Non-dispersive infrared
Nitrogen oxide (NO^2)	Annual average 0.05 ppm 24-hour average 0.08 ppm Hourly average 0.15 ppm	Chemiluminescent

Particulates:
  Total suspended particulates
  (TSP)
	Annual average 150 µg/m^3
	24-hour average 300 µg/m^3
		Beta-ray absorption
		High volume air sampler

Particulate matters (PM-10)	Annual average 80 µg/m^3 24-hour average 300 µg/m^3	
Ozone (O^3)	8-hour average 0.06 ppm Hourly average 0.1 ppm	Beta-ray absorption
Lead (Pb)	three-month average 1.5 µg/m^3	Atomic absorption spectrophotometry

Source: MOE Web site, *www.me.go.ka* (September 2000).

fensive odor, volatile organic compounds, ozone, and acid rain.

As the number of registered motor vehicles exceeded 11 million in 1999, they have become the main sources of air pollution. In Seoul, motor vehicles produce approximately 85 percent of the city's air pollution emissions, compared with 55 percent in 1991. Commercial vehicles such as buses and trucks account for only 4 percent of total motor vehicles but generate 47 percent of all air pollution emissions. Government measures to reduce motor vehicle pollution include development and commercialization of natural gas buses. The government plans to have 5,000 CNG (compressed natural gas) buses operating in eight cities by 2002 when the World Cup soccer games are held in Korea.

According to 1999 statistics, motor vehicles emitted 1.8 million tons of air pollutants, accounting for 41 percent of total volume of air pollutants generated (4.4 million tons). In particular, motor vehicles account for 89 percent of total carbon monoxide emission and 88 percent of hydrocarbon emission. Other sources of air pollution are industry (27 percent), power generation (17 percent), and heating (6 percent).

Korea's environmental standards for air pollution control have been established to conform to the standards recommended by the World Health Organization (WHO).

Air pollution control standards were introduced in 1979 when those for sulfur dioxide were established. Standards for carbon monoxide, nitrogen dioxide, suspended particulate, ozone, and hydrocarbon were added in 1983, and those for lead in 1991. In 1993, the government drafted and began to enforce more stringent standards. At the same time, new standards for particulate matters were adopted as the number of motor vehicles increased very rapidly, while those for hydrocarbon were excluded from the list.

Infrastructure Development

Both government and industry operate the following air quality monitoring systems:

- **Air pollution monitoring stations (telemetering systems):** Environmental management offices and local governments operate air pollution monitoring stations to monitor six major pollutants on a continuous basis. All monitored data are transmitted in real time to the EMO and the Ministry of Environment through telemetering systems (TMS). A total of 142 TMSs operate in 49 cities nationwide, of which 101 are managed by MOE and 41 by local governments.

- **Air pollution monitoring vehicles:** In the areas where telemetering systems are not installed or other special areas, EMOs operate monitoring vehicles to monitor air pollution. Currently, the EMOs operate eight vehicles.
- **Acid rain monitoring stations:** Since 1983, EMOs have operated acid rain monitoring stations to monitor rain acidity. Currently, 95 monitoring stations operate in 48 cities.
- **Smokestack telemetering systems:** Emitting companies began to install smokestack systems in the Ulsan industrial area in 1986. Smokestack systems continuously measure particulate, SOx, NOx, NH3, HCl, HF, and CO to produce measured data every five minutes. In 1999, 188 companies operated the smokestack systems. In Ulsan and Yochon, 89 companies operate 444 systems on 262 smokestacks according to administrative orders. In addition, 99 other large facilities such as cement plants and power plants operate 673 systems on 359 smokestacks in compliance with administrative recommendations. In the special industrial areas of Yochon and Ulsan Onsan, telemetering system control centers have been built with a total budget of $5.5 million and the centers are now in test operation. Starting in 2000, a new control center is being built for the capital zone surrounding Seoul. MOE allocated $3.7 million to this new project for 2000.

Market Size, Competitive Situation, and Market Opportunities

Unlike the water-wastewater and solid waste sub-sectors, Korea's market for air pollution control is driven by increasing investments in the private sector as the government enforces more demanding regulations. According to the Bank of Korea's environmental data for 1999, industries accounted for 91.8 percent of the nation's total environmental spending, compared with 3.2 percent for the government and 5.0 percent for households. The size of the market for all air pollution control products and services was estimated to be $1.13 billion in 1999, up 21 percent from $930 million in 1998. In 2000, this market is expected to reach $1.2 billion.

In the 1990s, the industry sector's investment in air pollution control continued to increase, reaching $733 million in 1997 but declining precipitously to $446 million in 1998 during the economic crisis. In 1999, investments in air pollution control facilities by industry expanded by 26 percent to reach $562 million as Korean companies needed to install or upgrade air pollution control equipment to meet the more demanding regulatory requirements. In 1999, Korean industries also increased their spending on managing and maintaining their air pollution control equipment by approximately 15 percent: from $414 million in 1998 to $475 million in 1999. Thus the total size of the industrial-sector market for air pollution control grew 20.6 percent from $860 million in 1998 to $1.04 billion in 1999.

In the public sector, the great majority of investment spending in air quality management has been made in building and maintaining air pollution monitoring systems and TMS control centers for smokestack telemetering systems. Starting in 2000, the Ministry of Environment secured a budget to support industries in purchasing CNG buses and building CNG stations in an effort to reduce automobile emissions. MOE plans to have 20,000 units of CNG buses and 210 CNG stations operating by 2007. MOE's budget for subsidy and loans is allocated at $30.4 million to support 1,500 CNG buses and 30 stations. MOE's 2000 budget for air quality monitoring systems is $5 million.

According to MOE and the Korea Institute of Science and Technology (KIST), Korea's technological capability in air pollution control is estimated to range from 30 percent to 70 percent, depending on the level of sophistication in each specific field of technology, given that the comparable capability of advanced nations, including the United States, is 100 percent. Korean air pollution control technology has improved to the extent that local manufacturers are now able to fabricate unsophisticated equipment such as bag filters and cyclone collectors. But the Korean industry still relies on foreign technologies in sophisticated fields. In the 1990s, more than 30 foreign companies transferred their air pollution control technologies to Korean companies. Japanese, U.S., and German companies have been most active in this field. Major areas of such technology transfer agreement include multicyclones, electrostatic precipitators, dust collectors, and desulfurization.

According to the Korea Environment Industry Association, around 570 companies are active in Korea's market for air pollution control, of which 169 firms specialize only in the air pollution control field. Main areas of air pollution control technology and equipment required by Korean industries include crude oil desulfurization, other industrial desulfurization, and exhaust gas treatment. The leading specialist firm in this field is Korea Cottrell, which has produced air pollution control equipment since the 1960s. Although most Korean equipment manufacturers can produce only low-tech products, this company can produce electrostatic precipitators. Other firms that produce electrostatic precipitators include Korea Heavy Industry, Halla Heavy Industry, and Hyundai Heavy Industry.

As Korea's major industries increase business activities and more stringent regulations are enforced, Korean companies will need to increase their investments in air pollution control in the process of expanding or upgrading their facilities. For U.S. suppliers of air pollution control equipment, large manufacturing companies affiliated with major conglomerates, such as Hyundai, Samsung, LG, and SK, and the state-run Korea Electric Power Corporation will continue to be the main target customers. U.S. engineering companies will find licensing opportunities with leading Korean general and specialized environmental engineering and construction firms. Main areas of air pollution control where the industry still lacks technological capability include flue gas and fuel desulfurization/denitrification, high-efficiency dust collectors, motor vehicle emission reduction, and air quality measuring devices. Korea's main industries that need advanced air pollution control equipment and operational technology include petrochemicals, power generation, automobile, electronics, and steel.

Chapter 8
Environmental Engineering and Consulting Services

The engineering and consulting services segment of Korea's environmental market is beginning to develop as a stand-alone business category. Under Korea's environmental laws, 17 business categories are classified as belonging to the environment industry. The categories that correspond to the environmental engineering and consulting services are "pollution control (or environmental) engineering and construction" and "environmental impact assessment (EIA) consulting." The ISO 14000 certification was introduced to Korea in 1996. Since then, more than 300 Korean companies have obtained this certification. Currently, nine Korean institutions are accredited to conduct environmental audits for the ISO 14000 certification, and some of them are affiliated with foreign organizations.

Environmental Engineering

Each engineering and construction contractor typically provides engineering services as part of the whole environmental project it undertakes. To date, no foreign engineering companies are licensed as prime contractors for pollution control projects. A few U.S. and European engineering companies, such as Black & Veatch, Bechtel, and Man GHH, operate branch offices in Korea. They provide environmental engineering services as part of a total engineering service package on sophisticated infrastructure and plant engineering projects such as civil, power generation, and petrochemical projects.

The pollution control industry is broken down into three sub-categories: air pollution, water pollution, and noise and vibration. According to 1998 data, there are 775 licensed pollution control contractors, of which 47 firms are registered for all the three fields. The Korean pollution control industry is dominated by general construction engineering contractors, and many of these contractors are subsidiaries of large conglomerates (chaebol) such as Hyundai, Samsung, LG, SK, Kolon, Hanhwa, and Doosan. These prime contractors typically conduct complex environmental projects through subcontracting arrangements with specialized engineering firms and/or equipment suppliers.

Foreign environmental engineering firms and equipment manufacturers usually participate in the Korean market for environmental infrastructure and other major private projects as subcontractors to large Korean companies or as technology transferrers in specialized fields. Although foreign firms have not been well-positioned as prime contractors for environmental projects, hundreds of foreign players have entered the environmental market through technology transfer. By 1996, a total of 227 cases of technology transfer were filed with the government as made from foreign sources. The accumulated license fees paid to foreign licensors amounted to approximately $90 billion. In the 1990s, 13 to 36 cases of foreign technology transfer were reported to the government each year until 1995.[1] Historically, Japanese firms have dominated Korea's market for foreign environmental technologies through all fields, including wastewater treatment, air pollution control, and waste incineration, with an estimated share of 40 to 50 percent. The United States is the second largest source of foreign environmental technology in Korea with around 20 percent of foreign share. European technology suppliers were not active in the Korean market in the past, but they have expanded their role and market share since the mid-1990s. The main European sources are Germany, France, and the United Kingdom. In particular, several European engineering firms have successfully entered Korea's expanding market for municipal incinerators in recent years, while U.S. firms have not been active in this growing market segment.

Korea's technological capability still depends largely on foreign sources, particularly in the fields of designing core equipment and parts, core end-of-pipe treatment, and preventive pollution control. The environmental industry has largely focused its efforts on adopting, operating, and applying foreign technologies, rather than making efforts to develop original technologies for components. Government efforts in technology development have been oriented toward environmental infrastructure construction, while advanced nations are developing next-

---

1. Foreign technology transfer data are not available for 1996 and thereafter as a result of the revision of the Foreign Capital Inducement Act of 1995 deregulating the notification requirement involving technology transfer arrangements.

generation technologies in the fields of environmental cleanup, restoration, and recycling. Since 1992, the government has executed a comprehensive environmental technology research and development program. Under this program, 192 R&D projects were conducted by 1999, of which 51 projects resulted in commercialization. So far, however, this program has not had much success with actual commercialization. The Ministry of Environment is continuing various policy efforts to develop practical technologies and promote the distribution and adoption of as many new domestic technologies as possible.

Environmental Impact Assessment

Approximately 120 engineering or consulting firms are licensed as Environmental Impact Assessment (EIA) consultants. They also conduct environmental feasibility studies for other infrastructure projects on behalf of national, regional, and local governments and other public organizations. In order to be qualified as an EIA consultant, a company must register with one of the environment management offices or regional environmental management offices.

Registration requirements include technical manpower, facilities, and equipment, among others. In 1999, there were 143 EIA projects contracted, with a total of $13.7 million. Main EIA project categories are road construction (49 projects in 1999), urban development (26 projects), tourist complex development (13 projects), port development (10 projects), industrial estate development (nine projects), sports facility construction (eight projects), railroad development (six projects), and waste treatment facility construction (four projects). No foreign firm has yet been licensed as an EIA consultant in Korea.

EIAs are required for 17 development categories:

- Urban areas
- Industrial estates
- Energy
- Ports
- Roads
- Water resources
- Railroads
- Airports
- Rural residential areas
- Reclamation and land-filling
- Tourist complexes
- Sports facility construction
- Forest areas

- Designated areas
- Waste treatment facility construction
- Defense or military facility construction
- Mining of soil, stones, sand, pebbles, and minerals

Environmental Audit (ISO Series)

The ISO certification system was introduced into Korea in 1993 when the Quality Management Promotion Act was enacted and enforced. In 1996, the ISO 14000 certification was adopted with the Act on the Promotion of Environment-Friendly Industry Structure. Initially, the Ministry of Commerce, Industry, and Energy (MOCIE) was responsible for the ISO accreditation. In 1997, the accreditation role was commissioned to the Korea Accreditation Board (KAB). Currently, 31 institutions are accredited by KAB for ISO 9000, QS 9000, and/or ISO 14000 series. Among them, nine institutions qualify for the ISO 14000 environmental management certification. As Korea's economy and industries depend heavily on international markets, leading companies have actively adopted the ISO 14000 as well as the ISO 9000. Since 1996, KAB issued 309 certificates of ISO 14000 series by the end of 1999, and the number continues to increase.

Market Opportunities

Korea has been a production-oriented country. Products are usually defined in terms of "hardware" only, and "software" (such as technical information and services) is not regarded as something that has a separate value apart from the product. Software costs are usually expected to be included in the hardware cost, and purchasers are reluctant to buy any software separately. But exceptions exist with high-tech engineering services required to design, build, and operate sophisticated facilities, such as nuclear power plants, petrochemical plants, and large-scale civil and environmental infrastructures.

In spite of such constraints, opportunities for advanced U.S. environmental technologies still exist in the public infrastructure construction sector due to the shortage of highly qualified Korean engineers. Main segments offering opportunities for U.S. engineering and other service firms include municipal incineration, hazardous waste treatment, and design of water and wastewater treatment facilities. From a long-term perspective, the Korean market offers greater growth potential with "preventive" environmental technologies, such as clean process design, ecological management and restoration, and sophisticated environmental information management systems than "end-of-pipe" technologies.

Opportunities for advanced U.S. technologies are emerging in the commercial sector as well. Many leading Korean manufacturing companies have already recognized that they need to approach their own environmental management issues in a proactive way to improve their corporate image as well as to avoid possible trade barriers related to environmental issues in major advanced international markets where more stringent environmental requirements exist. This trend will generate greater growth potential for environmental audit and management consulting services in the future.

Chapter 9
Positioning U.S. Exporters in Korea

United States exporters of environmental products and services who are new to the Korean market will most likely need to do a lot of preparatory work in planning and implementing market entry and business development strategies. Those who have already entered the Korean market will probably need to further develop their business in this market that offers long-term growth potential. They also need to assess more accurately and comprehensively the Korean market to continually take advantage of potential or emerging opportunities and to minimize any risk in expanding their commitments in the market.

As discussed in the previous sections, Korea seems to be one of the most attractive markets in the Asia-Pacific region in terms of market size and growth potential. But it is still one of the toughest international markets for a foreign company to do business with although entry barriers have been significantly eased in recent years. There still exist invisible barriers in various forms, such as cultural and communications gaps, inconsistency or obscurity in enforcing regulations, a possible need to adapt one's product to meet local technical standards, nationalistic sentiments, irregular or less-transparent practices compared to the U.S. standard, to name a few.

All these constraints in market knowledge and business practices require a U.S. exporter, whether it is new or has some local experience, to form a partnership with a competent and reliable Korean partner to succeed. U.S.-Korean partnership can be established by taking any of the following arrangements: agent or distributor agreement, technology transfer, and joint venture. If a U.S. company has substantial experience and knowledge in the Korean market, it can establish its own representative or branch office or a wholly owned subsidiary; acquiring an existing Korean company is also possible. A few U.S. and European environmental companies currently operate their branch offices in Korea, but there is no foreign company in the form of a wholly owned subsidiary. For foreign environmental companies, the most common forms of market entry into Korea are agent or distributor arrangements and technology transfer (or licensing).

A U.S. company interested in entering the Korean market or expanding its business in Korea should carefully review all major aspects of market attractiveness, competition, and its capability and resources to cope with any future challenges or risks. Based on these analyses, the company can objectively evaluate sales and profit potential and long-term sustainability and can form a winning market entry and positioning strategy. If one is not so sure of the possibility of long-term success and survival, direct exports through a distributor or agent will be the best mode of entry. By doing business with the right Korean partner, a U.S. exporter can learn more about local market situations and peculiarities.

In recent years, the Korean government has significantly eased requirements and procedures for foreign direct investment under the market opening and deregulatory initiatives. But actual foreign direct investments in the form of subsidiaries or joint ventures have not yet advanced in the environmental and construction engineering sectors. This is largely because entry barriers still exist, particularly in terms of local licensing and track record requirements as well as procedural transparency and nationalistic tendency in the bidding process for public projects. For U.S. environmental engineering and other service firms interested in public infrastructure projects, opportunities are emerging and growing to form joint ventures with major companies as the government has recently started to privatize parts of environmental infrastructure facilities such as waste and wastewater treatment facilities. A foreign company is now allowed to acquire all or part of equity shares in existing Korean companies. Thus, an acquisition strategy is also an alternative for a U.S. company to build or expand its business base in Korea. Tax incentives are available for foreign investors who bring in selected environmental and alternative energy technologies classified as "high-level technologies" according to the relevant regulation of the Foreign Investment Promotion Act.

Whatever mode of entry a U.S. company opts for, identifying the right partner or representative and building lasting mutual trust is critical to attaining long-term success in Korea. Although it is also important to prepare a clear-cut agreement, many Korean corporate decision-makers still place more value on personal trust and relationships than contractual terms and conditions. Such a trusting relationship can be built on maintaining frequent and effective communications, both formal and informal, and patience. In this context, it is also imperative to thoroughly evaluate the prospective partner(s) through reliable and objective sources in order to avoid or minimize any unexpected future conflicts and risks.

Chapter 10
Financing Programs and Resources

Key Agencies and Organizations

Recognizing the increasingly important role that U.S. environmental technologies and services play in infrastructure and industrial projects, several U.S. government agencies provide financing programs to assist U.S. companies in their environmental export activities. Several other international and regional development agencies, such as the World Bank and the Asian Development Bank (ADB), also provide trade and project financing in developing countries.

United States Department of Commerce (DOC)

DOC encourages, serves, and promotes the nation's international trade, economic growth, and technical advancement. DOC assists U.S. companies in targeting finance assistance programs and provides counseling on multilateral development bank operations, programs, and resources supporting exports of environmental technologies.

United States Agency for International Development (USAID)

USAID offers loans and grants on concessional terms to less developed countries for further development plans in eligible recipient countries. A variety of USAID programs help U.S. firms take advantage of international environmental market opportunities. Led by USAID, the United States-Asia Environmental Partnership (US-AEP) seeks to address Asia's environmental problems through the sharing and promotion of U.S. experience, technology, and practice. Private sector involvement is the key to this initiative. US-AEP coordinates the efforts of 25 U.S. government departments and agencies and thousands of business and non-governmental organizations.

Export-Import Bank (Ex-Im Bank)

To facilitate export, Ex-Im Bank offers financing support to foreign buyers of U.S. goods and services. Ex-Im Bank's loan guarantee and insurance programs help U.S. exporters compete in overseas environmental markets. Ex-Im Bank also holds regular seminars and group briefings on international finance and the organization's assistance programs.

Overseas Private Investment Corporation (OPIC)

OPIC encourages and assists U.S. private investment in eligible developing countries. It finances investments through direct loans and loan guarantees, provides political risk insurance, and offers investor advisory services. These programs, which must involve U.S. investment, are available for new environmental projects or expansion of existing facilities.

Small Business Administration (SBA)

SBA offers financial assistance, counseling, export workshops, and training for U.S. exporters. SBA helps firms enter international environmental markets by providing loans and loan guarantees for equipment, facilities, materials, working capital, and business development support for selected export market development activities. International trade officers located in districts throughout the United States can refer small businesses to SBA, state, and federal resources.

Trade and Development Agency (TDA)

TDA provides funding for pre-export studies and planning conducted by U.S. firms for major industrial, municipal, energy, and infrastructure projects. TDA supports U.S. environmental firms through feasibility studies, orientation visits and reverse trade missions, technical symposia, business conferences, training grants, and procurement information on major projects in developing and middle-income countries.

Financing, Investment, and Insurance Programs

Export-Import Bank of the United States (Ex-Im Bank) / Export Financing Hotline

Through its special toll-free number, the Ex-Im Bank provides information on its export credit insurance and pre-export financing through working capital guaranteed loans and medium- and long-term loans and guarantees to overseas buyers. Information is accessible through e-mail, from a fax system, on the Ex-Im Bank Internet home page, and on a bulletin board service. Ex-Im Bank offers briefing programs to the business community, including regular seminars and group briefings offered both at the Ex-Im Bank and at locations around the country.

Contact:
(800) 565-EXIM (3946),
(202) 565-3946 (Alaska, Hawaii, and
District of Columbia);
Fax retrieval: (800) 565-EXIM, press 1, press 2
E-mail: *bdd@exim.gov*
Internet: *http://www.exim.gov*

Ex-Im Bank / Environmental Export Programs

Ex-Im Bank is committed to increasing the level of support it provides to exporters of environmentally beneficial goods and services as well as to exporters participating in foreign environmental projects. Features of the program include the new short-term Environmental Export Insurance Policy and market-specific financing packages.

Contact:
Office of Business Development,
(202) 565-3939

Overseas Private Investment Corporation (OPIC) / Information Line

OPIC encourages U.S. businesses to invest in developing countries and emerging market economies to create U.S. jobs and exports and to promote economic growth at home and abroad. OPIC has led investment missions targeted directly at envirotech industries. The OPIC hotline responds to all preliminary inquiries or initial requests for information regarding OPIC programs and services, including investment insurance and finance programs.

Contact:
Information Officer, (202) 336-8799
Fax: (202) 408-5155;
Fax Retrieval: (202) 336-8700

OPIC / Global Environment Fund (GEF)

GEF seeks to find and invest in innovative companies and projects whose products, services, and technologies contribute actively to environmental improvement. In particular, the Global Environment Emerging Markets fund, a privately managed $70 million venture, seeks to invest in environmental companies and projects in emerging markets and developing countries. The fund especially seeks co-investment opportunities with established U.S. companies engaged in joint ventures and other operational partnerships with local firms serving environment-related industries in eligible emerging markets.

Contact:
H. Jeffrey Leonard, President,
Global Environment Management
Corporation, (202) 789-4500;
Fax: (202) 789-4508

Small Business Administration (SBA) / Business Loan Guarantee Program

Financing for fixed-asset acquisition or general working capital purposes may be obtained through SBA. The program encourages private lenders to make loans of up to $750,000 to borrowers who could not borrow on reasonable terms without government help.

Contact:
Office of Financial Assistance,
(202) 205-6570; fax: (202) 205-7064

SBA / Export Working Capital Program (EWCP)

The EWCP provides short-term financing to small businesses for export-related transactions. The SBA guarantees up to 90 percent of a secured loan or $750,000, whichever is less. Proceeds from the export sales are the primary source of repayment.

Contact:
Office of International Trade,
(202) 205-6720; fax: (202) 205-7064

SBA / Small Business Investment Companies (SBIC)

Licensed by SBA, firms whose investment strategies include export activities may receive equity capital or term working capital in excess of SBA's 750,000 statutory limit.

Contact:
Investment Division, (202) 205-6510;
fax: (202) 205-6959

U.S. Trade and Development Agency (TDA) / Environmental Projects

One of the most important sectors promoted by TDA is U.S. environmental technology goods and services. TDA's efforts include the funding of feasibility studies, orientation visits, training grants, and conferences. In addition, TDA has established trust funds at the World Bank and other multilateral development banks. These banks use TDA funds to hire U.S. consultants for projects being considered for financing by the multilateral banks.

Contact:
Environmental Project Manager,
(703) 875-4357; fax: (703) 875-4009

USAEP and the National Association of State Development Agencies (NASDA)/ The Environmental Technology Fund

An initiative of the United States-Asia Environmental Partnership (US-AEP) and the National Association of State Development Agencies (NASDA), the Environmental Technology Fund provides grants up to $20,000 to U.S. small and medium-sized businesses for the purpose of facilitating the transfer of environmental technologies to the Asia-Pacific region. Environmental activities eligible for a grant include technology workshops or seminars, focused business development missions, and technology or equipment demonstrations.

Contact:
Environmental Technology Fund
National Association of State
Development Agencies
750 First St. NE, Suite 701
Washington, DC 20002
(202) 898-1302; fax: (202) 898-1312

International Finance Corporation (IFC)

The IFC is unique compared with other multilateral financial institutions in that it lends directly to the private sector (as opposed to the government) of a developing country. There is no standard application procedure for obtaining IFC financing; companies must arrange for a meeting with a project officer or submit a preliminary proposal to the IFC.

Contact:
Environmental Division Manager,
(202) 473-0661

Development Project Opportunities

World Bank / Environmental Information Data Sheets

World Bank information on environmental projects to be undertaken around the world is available both on-line and at Public Information Centers. In addition, the World Bank lists projects that will be open for international competitive bidding and that are under consideration by the World Bank in its *Monthly Operational Summary.*

Contact:
World Bank Public Information Center,
(202) 458-5455; fax: (202) 522-1500;
Internet: *http://www.worldbank.org.* To
subscribe to the Monthly Operational
Summary, call (202) 473-1155 or fax
(202) 676-0581. For more information,
contact the Environmental Department
Director at (202) 473-3299.

World Bank / Global Environment Facility (GEF)

GEF is a multilateral lending organization managed by the World Bank for the United Nations Environment Program. It provides quarterly operational summaries of all upcoming and ongoing projects eligible for funding through GEF. These operational summaries are available quarterly through the GEF secretariat.

Contact:
GEF Secretariat, (202) 473-0508;
Internet: *http://www.gefweb.org*

Asian Development Bank (ADB)

The ADB awards projects through a competitive international bidding process. Announcements of project opportunities can be found in a biweekly United Nations' publication called *Development Business* or in *ADB Business Opportunities*. To subscribe to *Development Business,* call (212) 963-1515 or fax (212) 963-1381. To subscribe to *ADB Business Opportunities,* write:

Subscriptions–Information Office
c/o Asian Development Bank
ADB Avenue, Mandaluyong
Metro Manila, Philippines

Chapter 11
Government Export Assistance Programs

Key Agencies and Organizations

U.S. government agencies and departments actively support programs to help environmental firms compete and expand in the Asia-Pacific region, including Korea. The U.S. Agency for International Development (USAID), primarily through the U.S.-Asia Environmental Partnership (US-AEP), plays the largest role in providing technical assistance and promoting the transfer of environmental technologies to Korea. The Department of Commerce also plays a key role in promoting environmental technology exports. Other U.S. government agencies, including the Environmental Protection Agency (EPA), Department of Energy (DOE), and Small Business Administration (SBA), also have export promotion activities, but these are mostly in cooperation with USAID.

United States Agency for International Development (USAID) / U.S.-Asia Environmental Partnership (US-AEP)

The United States-Asia Environmental Partnership (US-AEP) is an interagency program led by USAID. US-AEP was established in 1992 to assist in addressing environmental degradation and sustainable development issues in Asia and the Pacific by mobilizing U.S. environmental experience, technology, and services. US-AEP's technology transfer activities are designed to fulfill some of Asia's environmental needs in a way that is mutually beneficial to Asian and American partners. Its technology transfer services include trade leads, business counseling, market research, grants, exchanges, and product promotion.

U.S. Department of Commerce (DOC)

DOC encourages, serves, and promotes the nation's international trade, economic growth, and technical advancement. DOC assistance in developing environmental markets includes industry and foreign market information, trade leads, technical information on export licenses and international standards, trade show and mission support, export counseling, and other business ad-

visory services. The International Trade Administration (ITA), DOC's division charged with foreign commercial operations, provides extensive assistance to help U.S. companies secure environmental market opportunities through U.S. and Foreign Commercial Service (US&FCS) trade specialists. The Environmental Technologies Exports (ETE) office is the principal contact within ITA that can link industry to programs and resources supporting exports of U.S. environmental technologies.

Environmental Protection Agency (EPA)

EPA's primary goal is to mitigate the adverse impacts of pollution on human health and the environment. EPA is one of the partner members of US-AEP. In addition to managing national environmental affairs, EPA helps U.S. firms take advantage of international environmental market opportunities.

U.S. Department of Energy (DOE)

DOE supports the administration's export promotion efforts to advance international commercial activities of U.S. energy firms. This effort spans a broad range of commercial, foreign policy, and technical assistance that already has involved thousands of U.S. companies throughout the energy sector. Assistance is provided in the following areas: natural gas, oil, and coal; electric power generation; alternative and renewable energy technologies; energy conservation, energy efficiency, and environmental technologies.

U.S. Small Business Administration (SBA)

SBA offers financial assistance, counseling, export workshops, and training for U.S. exporters. SBA helps firms enter international environmental markets by providing loans and loan guarantees for equipment, facilities, materials, working capital, and business development support for selected export market development activities. International trade officers located in districts throughout the United States can refer small businesses to SBA, state, and federal resources.

Environmental Export Assistance Programs

Environmental Technologies Industries (ETI) / International Trade Administration (ITA) / Department of Commerce

ETI serves as the primary point of contact for environmental technology export information and assistance at the Department of Commerce, in coordination with programs throughout the federal government. In addition to implementing the National Environmental Technologies Export Strategy, the ETI staff provide information on market research and trends; specific overseas market opportunities in the environmental sector; upcoming trade promotion events; and key contacts.

Contact:
Environmental Technologies Industries
ITA / Department of Commerce
1401 Constitution Ave., NW, Room 1003
Washington, DC 20230
(202) 482-1500; fax: (202) 482-5665
Internet: *www.environment.ita.doc.gov*

U.S. and Foreign Commercial Service (US&FCS) / ITA / Department of Commerce

The mission of the US&FCS is to support U.S. firms, especially small and medium-sized companies, in their efforts to increase exports. Located at U.S. embassies overseas, its Washington, D.C. headquarters, and district offices throughout the country, US&FCS offices maintain a worldwide service delivery network in the United States and 76 countries overseas. The global capabilities of US&FCS provide seamless service ranging from basic market research to arranging meetings with potential foreign buyers. Contact should be initiated through US&FCS district offices.

Contacts:
US&FCS Environmental Trade Programs
Department of Commerce
1401 Constitution Ave., NW, Room 3128
Washington, DC 20230
(202) 482-3922; fax: (202) 482-3159

Mitchel I. Auerbach, Commercial Attaché
U.S. Embassy / Commercial Service
82 Sejong-ro, Chongro-ku
Seoul 110-050, Korea

+82 (2) 397-4655; fax: +82 (2) 737-5357
Internet: *http://www.cskorea-doc.gov*

For the address and phone number of the nearest U.S. Department of Commerce district office, call (800) USA-TRADE(3) (800-872-8723). Internet: *http://www.ita.doc.gov/uscs*

United States-Asia Environmental Partnership (US-AEP) / USAID

US-AEP brings together the activities and resources of government, industry, and non-governmental institutions to offer U.S. exporters of environmental technology access to Asian market resources, including leads on environmental market opportunities, feasibility and pre-feasibility project assistance, and access to various grant and exchange programs. U.S. companies can also receive business counseling and training for employees and foreign customers. US-AEP currently works with governments and industries in 11 target economies: Korea, Hong Kong, India, Indonesia, Malaysia, Philippines, Singapore, Sri Lanka, Taiwan, Thailand, and Vietnam.

Contacts:
US-AEP Headquarters
United States
Mr. Peter Kimm
Executive Director
US-AEP/USAID
1300 Pennsylvania Ave., NW, 4th Floor
Washington, DC 20523 USA
(202) 712-4156; fax: (202) 216-3379
E-mail: usasia@usaep.org; web site: www.usaep.org

Asia
Mr. Dennis Zvinakis
Regional Director
RMC Building, 17th Floor
1680 Roxas Boulevard 1004
Malate, Manila, Philippines
(632) 522-4411, ext. 4460; fax: 632-521-5241
E-mail: *dzvinakis@usaid.gov*

Korea
Mr. Mitchel Auerbach,
Acting Director
Leema Building, Suite 1405
146-1, Susong-dong, Chongro-Ku
Seoul, Korea 110-140
+82 (2) 397-4114 or 397-4587; fax: +82 (2) 734-6559
E-mail: *Mitchel.Auerbach@mail.doc.gov* or *Je.Ha.Yang@mail.doc.gov*

Environmental Technology Network for Asia (ETNA) / US-AEP / USAID

The Environmental Technology Network for Asia (ETNA) is a U.S. government-sponsored clearinghouse that collects environmental trade leads from the Asia/Pacific region and disseminates them to U.S. environmental technology and services firms. Established in 1993, ETNA is an initiative of the United States-Asia Environmental Partnership (US-AEP) and the Global Technology Network (GTN) of the United States Agency for International Development (USAID). In cooperation with the U.S. Department of Commerce, US-AEP has placed Environmental Technology Representatives in 11 Asian countries to identify trade opportunities for U.S. companies and coordinate meetings between potential Asian and U.S. business partners. These environmental trade specialists meet regularly with decision-makers in industry and government in order to prepare concise trade leads that identify Asian buyers, environmental concerns, and proposed technology solutions. These leads are forwarded to ETNA, where they are matched against a database of over 2,700 registered U.S. companies, and then faxed to those companies that provide the requested technology or service. ETNA also provides business counseling to U.S. environmental companies interested in expanding into Asia, and provides market trend analysis on each providing country. Any U.S.-owned environmental firm is eligible to receive free trade leads. Companies may register online, or they may contact ETNA to register.

Contact:
Environmental Technology Network for Asia
US-AEP
1720 Eye St. NW, Suite 700
Washington, DC 20006, USA
(800) 818-9911; fax: (202) 835-8358
Internet: *http://www.usaep.org/ouractiv/etna.htm*

Office of International Activities (OIA) / U.S. Environmental Protection Agency (EPA)

OIA serves as EPA's principal point of contact on international environmental matters with other federal agencies and international organizations such as US-AEP or INFOTERRA, the United Nations Environmental Program's environmental information-sharing network. In this capacity, EPA disseminates key information on vendors, implementation of environmental regulations, regional environmental initiatives, and sound governmental technologies through its extensive collection of manuals, directories, clearinghouses, and databases. Foreign companies can contact EPA for directories and databases on U.S. companies offering environmental technologies and services. OIA also oversees the EPA's international travel and visitors programs, which often serve as a springboard for building or strengthening environmental institutions abroad and set the foundation for mutually beneficial future exchanges.

Contact:
Asia Program Manager
U.S. Environmental Protection Agency
401 M St., SW
Washington, DC 20460
(202) 564-6447; fax: (202) 260-3923

Appendix A
Major Environmental Projects in Korea

Table A.1   Major Municipal Sewage Treatment Projects

Regional government	Local government	Plant name (Location)	New or expansion	Starting	Ending	Capacity (in thousand tons per day)	Estimated Value (millions of won)
Seoul	Seoul	Kayang	Expansion	2001	2005	850	271,400
Seoul	Seoul	Chungrang	Expansion	2002	2005	710	209,450
Pusan	Pusan	Nambu	Expansion	2001	2005	244	118,096
Kwangju	Kwangju	Songdae	Expansion	2001	2005	215	104,060
Taejon	Taejon	Bongsan	Expansion	2001	2005	300	145,200
Kyonggi-do	Suwon	Suwon	Expansion	2002	2005	220	153,400
Chungchongnam-do	Sochon	Janghang	New	2000	2004	50	104,060
Kyongsang nam-do	Masan	Masan	Expansion	2001	2005	100	121,000

Note: Funding sources are the national government and the regional government. Part of national government funding derives from the Asian Development Bank and is provided in the forms of subsidies or loans.

Source: Environmental Management Research Center, *1999 Environmental Industry Yearbook* (Seoul, December 1999).

Table A.2   Major Industrial Wastewater Treatment Projects

Region	Location	Capacity (tons per day)	Total value (millions of won)	Government funding (millions of won)	Loan (millions of won)	Private funding (millions of won)	Timing
Taegu	Taegu Songseo	40,000	23,140	—	9,323	13,859	1996–1997
Kyonggi-do	Hwasung Palan	30,000	27,000	13,500	—	13,500	2000–2002
Chungchong buk-do	Chongju Ochang	63,000	64,063	26,145	—	37,918	1997–2002
Chollanam-do	Kunjang Kunsan	56,000	50,400	25,200	—	25,200	2000–2002
Chollanam-do	Yeochon	35,000	31,500	15,750	—	15,750	2000–2002
Chollanam-do	Yeochon Yulchon	33,000	29,700	14,850	—	14,850	1999–2002

Source: Environmental Management Research Center, *1999 Environmental Industry Yearbook* (Seoul, December 1999).

Table A.3   Major Wide Area Municipal Water Supply and Industrial Water Supply Projects

Category	Project Name	Capacity (thousands of tons per day)	Estimated value (billions of won)	Timing	Municipalities or estates supplied
Wide Area Municipal Water	South Chungnam	80	100	2001–2006	4
	West Chungnam	250	215	2001–2006	4
	West Kyongnam	100	112	2001–2006	4
	South Chonbuk	40	181	2001–2006	2
	Daechong Dam (III)	300	232	2002–2008	5
	Pohang area	150	123	2003–2006	2
	North Chonnam	60	—	2006–2011	2
	Capital zone (VII)	500	343	2006–2011	7
	Chonju area (II)	300	188	2006–2011	5
	West Kyongbuk	100	104	2006–2011	2
	Nam River Dam (III)	500	386	2006–2011	6
	Kumi area (III)	100	901	2008–2011	3
Industrial Water	Kadokdo	100	78	2001–2006	Pusan kadokdo
	Shihwa (I)	400	80	2002–2006	Shihwa, Panwol
	Asan (III)	500	320	2003–2006	Asan Bay estates
	Kunjang (II)	350	242	2003–2006	Kunjang
	Youngsanho	200	78	2003–2006	Samho, Youngam
	Kwangyang (IV)	200	142	2003–2007	Yeochon, Yulchon
	Shihwa (II)	900	334	2008–2011	Shihwa II, Ansan-shi

Source: Environmental Management Research Center, *1999 Environmental Industry Yearbook* (Seoul, December 1999).

Appendix B
U.S. Commercial Service Environmental Team Members in Korea

American Embassy
Commercial Service
82 Sejong-ro, Chongro-ku
Seoul 110-050, Korea

Contact:
Mr. Robert Dunn, Commercial Attaché
Tel: +82 (2) 397-4743; fax: +82 (2) 739-1628

United States-Asia Environmental Partnership (US-AEP)
Office of Technology Cooperation—Korea
c/o American Embassy
Commercial Service
82 Sejong-ro, Chongro-ku
Seoul 110-050, Korea
Tel: +82 (2) 397-4537; fax: +82 (2) 739-1628

Appendix C
In-Country Contacts

Korean Government and Quasi-Governmental Organizations

Mr. Insu Lee
Director General for International Cooperation
Ministry of Environment, Republic of Korea
Government Complex Kwacheon
1 Chungang-Dong, Kwacheon, Korea
Tel: +82 (2) 504-9238; fax: +82 (2) 504-9206
E-mail: *islee@moenv.go.kr*

Mr. Hag-Sig Son
General Manager, Commercial and Living Energy Division
The Korea Energy Management Corporation
3001-1 Pungdukchun-Ri, Suji-Eup, Yongin-Si, Kyonggi-Do, 449-840, Korea
E-mail: *hsson@kemco.or.kr*

Mr. Noh, Jong-Whan
General Manager, Center for Climate Change Mitigation
The Korea Energy Management Corporation
3001-1 Pungdukchun-Ri, Suji-Eup, Yongin-Si, Kyonggi-Do, 449-840, Korea
Tel: +82 (2) 2604-520; fax: +82 (2) 2604-529
E-mail: *jwnoh@kemco.or.kr*

Mr. Hong-Suk Hwang
Chairman
Environmental Management Corporation
4-15 Nonhyun-Dong, Kangnam-Ku,
Seoul, 135-010, Korea
Tel: +82 (2) 5190-111/3; fax: +82 (2) 5190-110
E-mail: *hshwang@emc.or.kr*

Mr. Jong-Suk Kim
Executive Director
Environmental Management Corporation
4-15 Nonhyun-Dong, Kangnam-Ku,
Seoul, 135-010, Korea
Tel: +82 (2) 519-0116; fax: +82 (2) 5190-110
E-mail: *jskim@emc.or.kr*

Mr. Do, Myung-Jung
Assistant Mayor for Environmental Management
Seoul Metropolitan Government, Korea
38 Seosomun-Dong, Chung-Ku, Seoul, 100-110, Korea
Tel: +82 (2) 771-4920/1; fax: +82 (2) 3707-9509

Mr. Chun-Koo Cho
Auditor
Korea Resources Recovery and Reutilization Corporation
Ssangma Building
24-5 Yoido-Dong, Youngdeunpo-Gu, Seoul, 150-010, Korea
Tel: +82 (2) 3773-9160 or 780-4652; fax: +82 (2) 783-5232

Dr. Ahn, Key-Hee
Director General, Policy Evaluation Bureau
National Assembly of the Republic of Korea
1 Yoido-Dong, Youngdeungpo-Ku, Seoul, 150-010, Korea
Tel: +82 (2) 788-2899 or 783-9811;
fax: +82 (2) 784-3384

Mr. Kang, Kyong-Shik,
Member
National Assembly of the Republic of Korea
1 Yoido-Dong, Youngdeungpo-Ku, Seoul, 150-010, Korea
Tel: +82 (2) 784-2516; fax: +82 (2) 788-3223

Dr. Park, Seh-Jik,
Member
National Assembly of the Republic of Korea
1 Yoido-Dong, Youngdeungpo-Ku, Seoul, 150-010, Korea
Tel: +82 (2) 784-1526; fax: +82 (2) 788-3502

Mr. Chung, Hyung-Keun
Member
National Assembly of the Republic of Korea
1 Yoido-Dong, Youngdeungpo-Ku, Seoul, 150-010, Korea
Tel: +82 (2) 784-2182; fax: +82 (2) 788-3506

Mr. Kim, Moo-Sung,
Member
National Assembly of the Republic of Korea
1 Yoido-Dong, Youngdeungpo-Ku, Seoul, 150-010, Korea
Tel: +82 (2) 784-5274; fax: +82 (2) 788-3420

Col. Yang, Im-Suk
Director, Environmental Division
Ministry of National Defense
3-Ga, Yongsan-Dong, Yongsan-Ku, Seoul, 140-701, Korea
Tel: +82 (2) 748-5860; fax: +82 (2) 748-5819

Mr. Ann, Chong-Hwan
Assistant Director, Foreign Procurement Division
Supply Administration, Republic of Korea
502-3, Banpo-Dong, Seocho-Ku, Seoul, 137-756, Korea
Tel: +82 (2) 533-0822/4; fax: +82 (2) 592-4475

Mr. Deok-Gil Rhee
Director, Water Quality Research Department
National Institute of Environmental Research
613-2 Bulkwang-Dong, Eunpyung-Ku, Seoul, 122-706,
Korea
Tel: +82 (2) 389-8722; fax: +82 (2) 357-2961

Dr. Jae-Hyung Kim
Researcher, Waste Treatment Engineering Division
National Institute of Environmental Research
#404, 613-2 Bulkwang-Dong, Eunpyung-Ku, Seoul,
122-706, Korea
Tel: +82 (2) 389-6711, ext. 802; fax: +82 (2) 358-2961
E-mail: *kimjaeh@soback.kornet.nm.kr*

Mr. Dong-Kon Lee
General Manager, International Cooperation Department
Small and Medium Industry Promotion Corporation
24-3 Yoido-Dong, Youngdeungpo-Gu, Seoul, 150-010,
Korea
Tel: +82 (2) 769-6840; fax: +82 (2) 782-9702
E-mail: *dongklee@mail.smipc.or.kr*

Mr. Sang-Yong Kwak
Director, Foreign Investment Information Center
North Cholla Province
Local Administration Building #706
234-2, Gongduk-Dong, Mapo-Gu, Seoul, 121-756, Korea
Tel: +82 (2) 715-6366; fax: +82 (2) 715-6367
E-mail: *sykwak@fiic.or.kr*

Mr. Kim, Duk-Kyu
President
Korea Industrial Complex Corporation
Yu Han Yang Haeng Building
49-6 Daebang-Dong, Dongjak-Ku, Seoul, 156-754, Korea
Tel: +82 (2) 828-1800/1; fax: +82 (2) 828-1810

Mr. Ik-Beom Park
Environment Research Team
**Kyonggido Institute of Health and Environment
Research**
324-1, Pajang-Dong, Jangan-Gu, Suwon, Kyonggi-Do,
Korea
Tel: +82 (2) 250-2581/3; fax: +82 (2) 250-2630
E-mail: *parkib@mail.provin.kyonggi.kr*

Mr. Cha, Seung-Hwan
Director General, Han River Basin Water Authority
Ministry of Environment
11th Floor, Hyundai Bescore Building
532 Kojan 1-Dong, Ansan City, Kyonggi-Do, 425-705,
Korea
Tel: +82 (2) 7902-405; fax: +82 (2) 7902-439

Korean Environmental Companies

Mr. Lee, Bae-Soo
General Manager, Environmental Technology Department
Korea Power Engineering Company, Inc.
360-9, Mabuk-Ri, Kusong-Myon, Yongin-Si, Kyounggi-Do,
449-713, Korea
Tel: +82 (2) 289-3270; fax: +82 (2) 289-4519
E-mail: *baesool@ns.kopec.co.kr*

Mr. D.W. Kim
General Manager, Research and Development Center
Samsung Engineering Co., Ltd.
266-2, Bojung-Ri, Kusung-Myun, Yongin-Si, Kyunggi-Do,
449-910, Korea
Tel: +82 (2) 263-2560 or +82 (2) 3458-3650; fax: +82 (2)
263-2561/2

Mr. Keun-Ho Choe
Team Leader, New Turn Team
Research and Development Center
Samsung Engineering Co., Ltd.
266-2, Bojung-Ri, Kusung-Myun, Yongin-Si, Kyunggi-Do,
449-910, Korea
Tel: +82 (2) 263-2549 or +82 (2) 3458-3509; fax: +82 (2)
263-2561/2
E-mail: *khchoe@samsung.co.kr*

Mr. Jong-Wan Choi
Executive Director, Industrial System and Machinery
Business
Samsung Heavy Industries Co., Ltd.
6th Floor, Dongam Tower
890-25 Dachi-Dong, Kangnam-Ku, Seoul, 135-280, Korea
Tel: +82 (2) 3458-6466; fax: +82 (2) 3458-6493

Dr. Daekyoo Hwang
Technical Director, Geoenvironmental Engineering and
Landfill Project
LG Construction Co., Ltd.
537 Namdaemun-Ro 5-Ga, Joong-Ku, Seoul, 100-722,
Korea
(C.P.O. Box 8345, Seoul, Korea)
Tel: +82 (2) 771-2645 or 728-2020; fax: +82 (2) 728-2556
E-mail: *lg60464@mail.const.lg.co.kr*

Dr. Joon Y. Sung
Managing Director, Research and Development Center for
Safety, Health and Environment
LG Corporate Institute of Technology
3rd Floor, Yonsei Engineering Research Center
134, Sinchon-Dong, Seodaemun-Ku, Seoul, 120-749, Korea
Tel: +82 (2) 364-8051; fax: +82 (2) 364-8053
E-mail: *jysung@lgcit.com*

Dr. Woon-Young Yoon
Senior MTS, Research and Development Center for
Environment, Safety and Health
LG Corporate Institute of Technology
Yonsei Engineering Research Center
134 Sinchon-Dong, Seodaemun-Ku, Seoul, 120-749, Korea
Tel: +82 (2) 364-2900, ext. 126; fax: +82 (2) 364-8054
E-mail: *wyyoon@lgcit.com*

Mr. Choi, Hong
Managing Director, Plant Marketing
SK Engineering and Construction Co., Ltd.
192-18, Kwanhun-Dong, Chongro-Ku, Seoul, 110-300,
Korea
(K.P.O. Box 222)
Tel: +82 (2) 3700-9280; fax: +82 (2) 3700-8410

Mr. Kee-Won Park
Technical Advisor
**Hyundai Industrial Development and Construction Co.,
Ltd.**
87 Samsung-Dong, Kangnam-Gu, Seoul, 135-090, Korea
Tel: +82 (2) 544-3794; fax: +82 (2) 519-9450
E-mail: *keewpark@shinbiro.com*

Mr. Sang-Chun Nam
Managing Director
Hyundai Industrial Development Construction Co., Ltd.
87 Samsung-Dong, Kangnam-Gu, Seoul, 135-090, Korea
Tel: +82 (2) 519-9671; fax: +82 (2) 519-9450

Mr. Yeon-Jeong Lim
General Manager, Environmental Project Team, Plant
Division
Daewoo Corporation, Engineering and Construction
C.P.O. Box 8269, Seoul, 100-095, Korea
Tel: +82 (2) 2259-5165; fax: +82 (2) 2259-3916 or
2259-3913
E-mail: *7726418@mail.dwconst.co.kr*

Mr. P.T. Kim
President
Green Resources Co., Ltd.
Hyoungjin Building #301
61-1, Sogyo-Dong, Mapo-Gu, Seoul, 121-210, Korea
Tel: +82 (2) 3143-0943 or 3143-0944;
fax: +82 (2) 3141-6810

Mr. Hong-Kyun Rhee
President
Bomon Corp.
Rm. #508, Tae-A Building
1309-11, Sucho-Dong, Socho-Gu, Seoul, 137-070, Korea
Tel: +82 (2) 566-4194; fax: +82 (2) 564-4609
E-mail: *bomoon@bora.dacom.co.kr*

Mr. Yoon, Yong-Jin
Chairman
C&G Korea, Inc.
371-19 Shinsu-Dong, Mapa-Gu, Seoul, 121-110, Korea
Tel: +82 (2) 718-0456; fax: +82 (2) 718-0457

Mr. Lee, Chong-Gak
President
Geosung Development Co., Ltd.
Daeyun Building #508
869-12, Bongchun 4-Dong, Gwanak-Ku, Seoul, 151-054,
Korea
Tel: +82 (2) 872-6611; fax: +82 (2) 872-6616

Mr. Keum-Young Lee
President
Keumsung Environmental Development
2nd Floor Subbong Bldg., 76-22 Gochurk-Dong, Kuro-Ku,
Seoul, 152-080, Korea
Tel: +82 (2) 614-0014; fax: +82 (2) 614-0013

Mr. H.M. Kim
President
Con-Tech Corporation
2nd Floor, Maru Building
86-7 Nonhyun Dong, Kangnam-Ku, 135-010, Korea
Tel: +82 (2) 512-2482/3 or 517-7708/9; fax: +82 (2)
549-4991
E-mail: *hmkim@contech.co.kr*; Web site: *www.contech.co.kr*

Mr. David S. Ahn
Vice President
Environmental Resources Management
Suite 905, Marine Center Building
118 Namdaemun-Ro 2-Ga, Chung-Ku, Seoul, 100-706,
Korea
Tel: +82 (2) 752-7141/3; fax: +82 (2) 752-7114
E-mail: *davidahn@nuri.net*

Mr. Kevin Park
President
NGV International Inc.
178, Anbo-Ri, Seo-Myun, Chuncheon-Si, Kangwon-Do,
200-835, Korea
Tel: +82 (502) 777-2900 or +82 (361) 263-6465; fax: +82
(361) 263-6464

Mr. Brett Song
Senior Director
U.S. Filter–Korea
47th Floor, 63 Daehan Life Insurance Building
60 Yoido-Dong, Youngdeungpo-Ku, Seoul, 150-763, Korea
Tel: +82 (2) 789-6666; fax: +82 (2) 782-3264
E-mail: *brett@mail.hitel.net*

Mr. Wendell E. Moon Jr.
General Manager
ECG, Inc./Pacific Division
#1-1005 Mirinae
Bongduk 3-Dong, San 89-3, Nam-Ku, Taegu, 705-023, Korea
Tel: +82 (53) 622-1580; fax: +82 (53) 653-9084
E-mail: *moonw@ecgcom.com*

Mr. Peter D. Kim
Managing Director–Korea
CDM International, Inc.
13th Floor, CBS Building
917-1 Mok-Dong, Yangchun-Ku, Seoul, 158-701, Korea
Tel: +82 (2) 555-7690; fax: +82 (2) 555-7690
E-mail: *pdkim@cdm.com.kr*

Mr. Hamm, Jung-Woong
Chairman
Taegu Dyeing Industrial Center
402-2 Pyongri-Dong, Seoul, Taegu, Korea
Tel: +82 (53) 355-1521/3; fax: +82 (53) 354-0103

Dr. Myoung-Cho Yoon
President
Korea Environmental Research, Inc.
Woojin Building #301
1022-1 Bangbae 3-Dong, Socho-Ku, Seoul, 137-063, Korea
Tel: +82 (2) 588-8435; fax: +82 (2) 588-8463
E-mail: *keric@chollian.net*

Mr. Hong, Young-Kil
President
Young Engineering Co., Ltd.
5th Floor, Yang Kyung Building
386-2 Magwon-Dong, Mapo-Gu, Seoul, 121-230, Korea
Tel: +82 (2) 326-0762; fax: +82 (2) 326-0762
E-mail: *younghyk@unitel.co.kr*

Mr. Dae-Gyu Lee
President
Kyung Gi Environmental Engineering and Equipment Co., Ltd.
395 Sanha-Ri, Wongok-Myun, Ansung-Si, Kyonggi-Do, 456-810, Korea
Tel: + (82) (333) 663-5617/8; fax: +82 (333) 663-5619

Mr. Hee-Tag Jun
Director, Planning and Development Office
Green World Co., Ltd.
140-1 Yangkyo-Ri, Osung-Myun, Pyongtaek City, Kyonggi-Do, 451-870, Korea
Tel: +82 (333) 682-4068; fax: +82 (333) 682-4068
E-mail: *kkseoul@choillian.net*

Mr. Choi, Hyun
President
Sam Duck Engineering Co., Ltd.
12BL 7LT Namdong Industrial Complex
622-6, Namchon-Dong, Namdong-Gu, Inchon, 405-100, Korea
Tel: +82 (32) 822-3100/5; fax: +82 (32) 822-3106

Mr. Man-Jae Lee
Vice President
Tech-Kor-Engineering Co., Ltd.
10th Floor, Kum Gang Building
14-35 Yoido-Dong, Youngdeungpo-Ku, Seoul, 150-010, Korea
(K.P.O. Box 1521)
Tel: +82 (2) 784-4383/7; fax: +82 (2) 784-2770
E-mail: *techkor@hitel.net*

Mr. Lee, Seung-Woo
Executive Director
Daekeum Industrial Co., Ltd.
720 Dohwa-Dong, Nam-Ku, Inchon City, Korea
Tel: +82 (32) 874-0211; fax: +82 (32) 874-0250
E-mail: *dk0211@daekeum.kr*

Academia

Dr. Kil-Choo Moon
Director, Environment Research Center
Korea Institute of Science and Technology
P.O. Box 131, Cheongryang
Seoul, 130-650, Korea
Tel: +82 (2) 958-5802/3; fax: +82 (2) 958-5805
E-mail: *kcmoon@kistmail.kist.re.kr*

Dr. Kim, Jong-Gook
Senior Research Fellow, Environmental Natural Resource Science
Korea Institute of Science and Technology
P.O. Box 131, Cheongryang
Seoul, 130-650, Korea
Tel: +82 (2) 958-6390; fax: +82 (2) 958-6868
E-mail: *jgkim@kistmail.kist.re.kr*

Dr. Hang-Sik Shin
Professor of Environmental Engineering
Department of Civil Engineering
Korea Advanced Institute of Science and Technology
373-1, Kusong-Dong, Yusong-Ku
Taejon, 305-701, Korea
Tel: +82 (42) 869-3613 or 869-3653; fax: +82 (42) 869-3610

Dr. Yu, Tae U
Director, Center for Cleaner Production
Korea Institute of Industrial Technology
35-3, Hongchun-Ri, Ibjang-Myun, Chongan-Si, 300-820,
Korea
Tel: +82 (417) 5608-501 or 5608-532;
fax: +82 (417) 5608-510
E-mail: *ytu@kitech.re.kr*

Dr. Yoon-Shin Kim
Professor of Environmental Health, College of Medicine
Hanyang University
17 Haengdang-Dong, Sungdong-Gu
Seoul, 133-791, Korea
Tel: +82 (2) 290-0692 or 290-8279; fax: +82 (2) 299-3915

Dr. Eung-Bai Shin
Professor, Civil Engineering Department
Hanyang University
17 Haengdang-Dong, Sungdong-Gu
Seoul, 133-791, Korea
Tel: +82 (2) 291-8089 or 290-0559; fax: +82 (2) 291-8089

Dr. Sang-Don Lee
Professor of Law, College of Law
Chungang University
Hukseog-Dong, Dongjak-Gu, Seoul, 156-756, Korea
Tel: +82 (2) 820-5434; fax: +82 (2) 816-6760

Dr. Sung-Hoon Park
Chief of Research Planning Department
Institute for Environmental Technology Industry
Pusan National University
San 30, Changjung-Dong, Keumjung-Gu, Pusan, 609-735,
Korea
Tel: +82 (51) 510-2395/1493; fax: +82 (51) 515-9769
E-mail: *shpark0@hyowon.pusan.an.kr*

Dr. Rae-Woong Chang
Director, Environment and Energy Research Division
Research Institute of Industrial Science and Technology
32 Hyojang-Dong, Nam-Ku, Pohang City, 790-300,
Kyungbuk, Korea
(P.O. Box 135 Pohang, 790-600, Korea)
Tel: +82 (562) 279-6017; fax: +82 (562) 279-6729
E-mail: *rwchang@risnet.rist.re.kr*

Dr. Soo-Saeng Kim
Environmental Problem Research Institute
Department of Environmental Engineering
Dong-A University
840 Hadan-Dong, Saha-Gu, Pusan, 604-714, Korea
Tel: +82 (51) 201-0917 or 200-7675; fax: +82 (51) 208-2232

Dr. Seongho Hong
Professor, Department of Chemical Engineering
College of Engineering
Soongsil University
1-1, Sangdo 5-Dong, Dongjak-Ku, Seoul, 156-743, Korea
Tel: +82 (2) 820-0628; fax: +82 (2) 812-5378
E-mail: *shong@saint.soognsil.ac.kr*

Dr. In-Sik Nam
Professor of Environmental Engineering
Pohang University of Science and Technology
San 31 Hyoja-Dong, Nam-Gu, Pohang-Si, Kyungbuk, 790-
784, Korea
Tel: +82 (562) 279-8302/5; fax: +82 (562) 279-8299
E-mail: *see@vision.postech.ac.kr*

American State Offices in Korea

Mr. Kyung-Sun Yang
Representative
Alaska State Office Representative for Korea
Suite 1329, Manhattan Building
36-2 Yoido-Dong, Youngdeunpo-Ku, Seoul, 150-549, Korea
Tel: +82 (2) 786-6921 or 761-2951; fax: +82 (2) 3775-3139
E-mail: *soakor@kotis.net*

Mr. Young-Min Lee
Representative
California Office of Trade and Investment
Leema Building, Suite 400
146-1, Susong-Dong, Chongro-Gu, Seoul, 110-755, Korea
Tel: +82 (2) 733-2341; fax: +82 (2) 733-1028 or 739-0905
E-mail: *ymlcoti@bora.dacom.co.kr*

Mr. Jong-Kook Park
Representative
State of Florida, Department of Citrus, Korea Office
Room 402, Union Building
961-3 Daechi 3-Dong, Kangnam-Ku, Seoul, 135-010, Korea
Tel: +82 (2) 561-2321; fax: +82 (2) 561-2322

Mr. Sung-Duck Oh
Director
Indiana State East Asian Office, Korea Liaison
A-511, Champs-Elysees Center
889-5, Daechi-Dong, Kangnam-Ku, Seoul, 135-280, Korea
Tel: +82 (2) 561-7901/2; fax: +82 (2) 561-7903
E-mail: *indiace@unitel.co.kr*

Mr. Keum-Dong Han
Director
State of Missouri Korea Office
Room 4201, Korea World Trade Center
159-1, Samsung-Dong, Kangnam-Gu, Seoul, 135-729, Korea
Tel: +82 (2) 551-3991/2; fax: +82 (2) 551-3993
E-mail: *mokorea@ktnet.co.kr*

Mr. Kim, Ji-Won
Director
Korea Representative Office, State of Oregon, USA
Suite 1301, Samkoo Building
Tel: +82 (2) 753-1349 or 755-1439; fax: +82 (2) 753-5154
E-mail: *jimwkim@chollian.net*

Mr. Kenneth S. Yang
Director
Commonwealth of Pennsylvania Korea Office
14th Floor, FKI Building
28-1 Yoido-Dong, Youngdeungpo-Gu, Seoul, 150-756,
Korea
Tel: +82 (2) 786-7701/3; fax: +82 (2) 786-7704
E-mail: *kensyang@soback.kornet21.net*

Mr. I. K. Kim
Director
State of Utah Korea Office
Suite 1201, Sung Jee Heights Building
702-13, Yoksam-Dong, Kangnam-Gu, Seoul, 135-080, Korea
Tel: +82 (2) 553-6829 or 568-8537; fax: +82 (2) 555-5230
E-mail: *ikkim@soback.kornet.nm.kr*

Dr. Sang-Min Woo
Commonwealth of Virginia
Virginia Port Authority, Korea Office
1512 Kyobo Building
1 Chongro 1-Ga, Chongro-Gu, Seoul, 110-714, Korea
Tel: +82 (2) 739-6248/9; fax: +82 (2) 739-6538
E-mail: *vpaseoul@chollian.net*

Mr. Hyun-Soo Kil
Director/President
Wisconsin Department of Commerce, Korea Office
Seoul Consulting International, Inc.
1301 Jindo Building
37 Dowha-Dong, Mapo-Gu, Seoul, 121-040, Korea
(M.P.O. Box 347, Seoul, Korea)
Tel: +82 (2) 702-6222, 702-4804/6; fax: +82 (2) 702-6036
E-mail: *kaybong@kotis.net*

Associations, NGOs, Magazines

Korean Environment Industry Association
Pungjeon Bldg., 11-3 Jung-dong, Chung-gu, Seoul, Korea
Tel: +82 (2) 774-0123; fax: +82 (2) 775-7043

Association of Foreign Trading Agents of Korea
Dongjin Bldg., 218 Hankangro 2-ga, Yongsan-gu, Seoul 140-012, Korea
Tel: +82 (2) 785-4373; fax: +82 (2) 785-4373

Mr. Choi, Yul
General Secretary
Korea Federation for Environmental Movement
251, Nooha-Dong, Chongro-Gu, Seoul, 110-042, Korea
Tel: +82 (2) 735-7000; fax: +82 (2) 730-1240
E-mail: *choiy@kfem.or.kr*

Mr. C. M. Yoo
Director, Administration Department
Korea Petrochemical Industry Association
6th Floor, Women's Mission Center
Yeonji-Dong, Chongro-Ku, Seoul, 110-738, Korea
Tel: +82 (2) 744-0116; fax: +82 (2) 743-1887

Mr. Kim, Dong-Hwan
Chief Editor
Korea Water Resources Environmental News
3rd Floor, Yunshin Building
336-21 Shinsa-Dong, Eunpyung-Ku, Seoul, 122-080, Korea
Tel: +82 (2) 308-2333; fax: +82 (2) 308-2335

Mr. Kim, Sang-Ha
President
Korea Chamber of Commerce and Industry
C.P.O. Box 25, Seoul, Korea
Tel: +82 (2) 777-8043; fax: +82 (2) 778-8169

Mr. Stephen A. Bowen
Research/Publication/IT Manager
American Chamber of Commerce in Korea
Suite 4501, Korea Trade Center
159-1 Samsung-Dong, Kangnam-Ku, Seoul, 135-731, Korea
Tel: +82 (2) 564-2040; fax: +82 (2) 564-2050
E-mail: *steve_bowen@amchamkorea.org*

Appendix D
Helpful Documents

Environmental Technologies Industries/Korea Industry Information
U.S. Department of Commerce, International Trade Administration
Web site: *http://infoserv2.ita.doc.gov/ete*
- Dioxin Emission Generated from Solid Waste Incineration in Korea
- Environmental Market Outlook for Korea
- Exim Expands Offerings in China, South Korea
- Incineration Ash Treatment Prospects in Korea
- Regional Environmental Projects in Korea
- Rivers and Reservoirs Clean-Up Project in Korea
- Volatile Organic Compound Technologies in Korea

Korea: Environmental Market Analysis
United States-Asia Environmental Partnership (US-AEP)
Web site: *http://www.usaep.org/export/em-korea-ema-v4.htm*
- Country Overview
- Market Estimates and Analysis
- Competition
- Regulatory Impact

Korea: Regulatory Framework
United States-Asia Environmental Partnership (US-AEP)
Web site: *http://www.usaep.org/export/em-korea-rf.htm*
- Regulations—Key National Legislation
- Institutions—Government Agencies
- The Policy Context—Enforcement and Compliance

Ministry of Environment (MOE), Republic of Korea
Web site: *http://www.me.go.kr/english*
- Green Korea 1999
- Basic Policy for Nature Conservation
- Environmental Vision of Korea
- Environmental Protection in Korea
- Second Mid-term Comprehensive Plan for Environmental Improvement
- National Action Plan for Agenda 21
- Toxic Chemicals Control Act, Its Enforcement Decrees and Regulations
- The Nature of Korea
- Korean Biodiversity Clearing-House Mechanism
- National Biodiversity Strategy
- Korea's Environmental Labeling Program
- ENVEX2000 Introduction
- Green Korea 2000

Appendix E
Miscellaneous Environmental Market Data

Table E.1   Average Exchange Rates, 1995–2001 (Korean won per U.S. dollar)

1995	1996	1997	1998	1999	2000(P)	2001-2002(P)
771.0	804.8	951.1	1,398.9	1,189.5	1,120	1,050

P – projected
Source: Bank of Korea (1995–1999).

Table E.2   MOE Budget by Environmental Sector, 1999 and 2000 (billions of won)

Sector	1999 Budget	2000 Budget	Change in Amount	Percent Change	Major Uses
Water supply management	241.6	244.2	2.6	1.1	• Developing and improving regional water supply plants
Water quality preservation and wastewater management	355.2	408.2	53.0	14.9	• Installing waste water treatment plants • Supporting industrial waste treatment projects
Waste management	268.7	286.5	17.9	6.6	• Developing landfills • Installing incineration plants • Installing recycling plants
Environmental R&D	114.0	126.7	12.7	11.1	• R&D of environmental technologies • Supporting funds for environmental improvement • Developing environmental research complexes
Natural environment preservation	59.2	72.9	13.7	23.2	• Pollution control for dead mines • National park management
Air quality preservation	9.5	46.2	36.7	386.8	• Supplying CNG buses • Expanding air quality monitoring network
General environmental management, other	105.5	115.0	9.5	9.0	
Total all sectors	**1,153.6**	**1,299.7**	**146.1**	**12.7**	

Source: Environmental Management Research Center, *1999 Environmental Industry Yearbook*, (Seoul, 1999).

Table E.3   Government Environmental Investments by Environmental Sector, 1995–1999 (billions of won)

Sector	1995	1996	1997	1998	1999 (P)
Air	4.2	9.5	9.9	11.1	10.0
Water and soil	1,339.3	1,552.4	2,246.6	1,761.9	1,882.2
Water	n.a.	n.a.	n.a.	1,756.2	1,877.7
Soil	n.a.	n.a.	n.a.	5.7	4.5
Waste	355.4	383.8	423.2	532.8	553.9
Collection and transport	n.a.	n.a.	n.a.	38.3	29.8
Treatment	n.a.	n.a.	n.a.	494.5	524.1
Noise and vibration	6.4	7.2	10.3	6.6	5.6
Other	26.2	22.6	23.8	17.0	15.8
Total	**1,731.5**	**1,975.5**	**2,713.9**	**2,329.5**	**2,467.5**

n.a. − not available

P − preliminary

Source: Bank of Korea, *1999 Environmental Expenditure (Preliminary)*, (Seoul, October 2000).

Table E.4   Industrial Environmental Investments by Environmental Sector, 1995–1999 (billions of won)

Sector	1995	1996	1997	1998	1999 (P)
Air	540.3	528.2	806.1	491.0	618.0
Water and soil	476.0	547.7	399.5	293.1	242.8
Water	n.a.	n.a.	n.a.	286.3	237.9
Soil	n.a.	n.a.	n.a.	6.8	4.9
Waste	268.5	345.8	256.9	180.5	189.7
Collection and transport	n.a.	n.a.	n.a.	22.4	22.0
Treatment	n.a.	n.a.	n.a.	158.2	167.7
Noise and vibration	32.0	31.9	9.8	6.3	7.4
Other	82.1	78.0	58.6	51.7	7.4
Total	**1,399.0**	**1,531.5**	**1,531.0**	**1,022.6**	**1,097.4**

n.a. − not available

P − preliminary

Source: Bank of Korea, *1999 Environmental Expenditure (Preliminary)*, (Seoul, October 2000).

Table E.5   Environmental Investments by Top 10 Korean Conglomerates, 1995–1998 (billions of won)

Conglomerate (Group)	1995	1996	1997	1998
Hyundai	251	483	198	127
Samsung	320	480	340	140
Daewoo	76	98	100	n.a.
LG	338	433	285	271
SK	377	330	70	93
Hanjin	n.a.	n.a.	n.a.	n.a.
Ssangyong	211	29	17	33
Hanwha	n.a.	n.a.	n.a.	n.a.
Kumho	51	56	51	48
Lotte	16	14	10	16

n.a. − not available

Source: Korea Environmental Industry Association.

Table E.6   Industry's Investments in Pollution Control by Industry Sector, 1996–1998 (billions of won)

Industry	1996	1997	1998
Food and beverage	85	87	42
Textiles	26	41	34
Pulp and paper	77	26	15
Chemicals	131	92	51
Oil refining	60	69	35
Rubber and plastics	16	15	9
Non-metal materials	73	57	31
Basic metals	142	190	51
Fabricated metals, machinery and equipment	131	58	47
Audiovisual and communications equipment	22	37	18
Electrical instruments and machinery	138	124	87
Transportation equipment	73	45	34
Other manufacturing	569	890	1,303
Total all industries	**1,540**	**1,731**	**1,758**

Source: Korea Environmental Industry Association.

Table E.7   Number and Amount of Pollution Control Projects by Sector, 1996–1998

	Sector	1996	1997	1998
Number of projects	Air	3,273	3,290	1,935
	Water quality	2,177	1,889	1,427
	Noise and vibration	440	449	352
	Total	**5,890**	**5,628**	**3,714**
Total amount of projects (in billions of won)	Air	547	670	905
	Water quality	916	1,002	790
	Noise and vibration	76	59	63
	Total	**1,540**	**1,731**	**1,758**

Source: Korea Environmental Industry Association.

Table E.8   Environmental Improvement Fees, 1996–1998 (millions of won)

Year	Number of Cases (in thousands)	Amount of Fees Imposed (a) (in millions of won)	Amount of Fees Collected (b) (in millions of won)	Rate of Collection (b)(a) (percent)
1996	5,527	178,380	157,724	88.4
1997	6,417	250,333	218,895	87.4
1998	6,756	320,566	267,280	83.4

Source: Environmental Management Research Center, *1999 Environmental Industry Yearbook,* (Seoul, December 1999).

Table E.9   Public Discharge Fees Collected, 1996–1998

Year	Total		Fees on Excess Discharges		Basic Fees	
	Cases	Amount (millions of won)	Cases	Amount (millions of won)	Cases	Amount (millions of won)
1996	3,190	11,928	3,190	11,928	—	—
1997	4,506	34,051	2,872	13,327	1,634	20,724
1998	4,935	45,810	2,230	15,512	2,705	30,298

Source: Environmental Management Research Center, *1999 Environmental Industry Yearbook,* (Seoul, December 1999).

Table E.10 Number of Pollution Control Contractors by Specialization 1998

All Contractors	Air	Water	Noise and Vibration	Air, Water, and Noise Vibration	Air and Water	Air and Noise Vibration	Water and Noise Vibration
775	169	372	29	47	155	2	1

Source: Environmental Management Research Center, *1999 Environmental Industry Yearbook,* (Seoul, December 1999).

Table E.11 Number of Pollution Control Contractors, by Size of Capitalization, 1998

	Total	1 billion or more won	500–999 million won	200–499 million won
Number	775	286	59	430
Percent	100	37.0	7.6	55.5

Source: Environmental Management Research Center, *1999 Environmental Industry Yearbook,* (Seoul, December 1999).

Table E.12 Government Financing for Private-Sector Pollution Control Projects, 1997–2001

	to 1996	1997	1998	1999	2000 (P)	2001 (P)
Total amount (in millions of won)	321,917	60,000	54,000	50,000	60,000	70,000
Number of projects financed	3,002	270	240	280	300	330

P – projected.

Note: Main fields of government financing include earthwork, installation of steel structures, and purchases and installation of environmental machinery, equipment, and instrumentation such as measuring instruments.

Source: Environmental Management Research Center, *1999 Environmental Industry Yearbook,* (Seoul, December 1999).

Table E.13   Top 30 Pollution Control Contractors (Engineering and Construction Companies), 1998

Rank	Company	Sector*	Total Value of Projects (millions of won)	Number of Projects
1	Korea Power Engineering (KOPEC)	A, NV, W	249,971	9
2	Namkwang Engineering and Construction	A, NV, W	98,264	10
3	Dongkwang Environment	A	94,201	12
4	Hyundai Industry Development and Construction	A, NV, W	84,398	3
5	Korea Heavy Industry Corporation	A, NV, W	72,316	7
6	Sungwon Industry Development and Construction	W	53,371	5
7	Lotte Engineering	A, NV, W	52,069	16
8	Samsung Engineering	A, NV, W	48,369	10
9	Ssangyong Engineering and Construction	A, NV, W	47,459	3
10	Sampoong Engineering and Construction	W	46,825	1
11	LG Engineering	A, NV, W	34,673	18
12	Daewon Engineering and Construction	W	28,970	1
13	Hyundai Precision and Industry	A, NV, W	28,021	4
14	Korea Cottrel	A	26,431	29
15	Hyundai Heavy Industry	A, NV, W	22,817	9
16	Kumho Engineering and Construction	W	21,191	20
17	Hanjin Engineering and Construction	A, NV, W	20,144	5
18	Lim Kwang Construction	A, NV, W	19,796	10
19	Dong-Ah Construction Industrial	A, NV, W	16,939	5
20	Daelim Engineering	A, NV, W	16,740	24
21	LG Industrial Systems	A, W	16,683	7
22	Kongyoung Engineering	A	15,993	26
23	Youngdo Construction and Industry	W	15,744	4
24	Dongsung Engineering and Construction	W	14,893	4
25	Hyundai Engineering	A, NV, W	12,675	4
26	Doosan Construction and Engineering	A, NV, W	12,124	6
27	Hyundai Engineering and Construction	A, NV, W	11,451	6
28	Dongbu Corporation	A, NV, W	10,678	6
29	Wonbang Tech	NV	10,513	15
30	Jindo Engineering and Construction	A, NV, W	10,359	8

*A: air; W: water; NV: noise and vibration.

Source: Environmental Management Research Center, *1999 Environmental Industry Yearbook*, (Seoul, December 1999).

Appendix F
Major Korean Environmental Companies

Engineering and Construction Companies

Korea Power Engineering Co., Ltd. (KOPEC) (General)
360-9, Mabuk-ri, Kusong-myon, Yongin-shi, Kyonggi-do
Tel: +82 (31) 289-3055; fax: +82 (31) 283-6215
Representative: Park, Sang-ki

Samsung Engineering Co., Ltd. (General)
946-1 Daechi-dong, Kangnam-gu, Seoul
Tel: +82 (2) 3458-3326; fax: +82 (2) 3458-4047
Representative: Yang, In-mo

International Construction Co., Ltd. (Water)
830-42, Bumil 2-dong, Dong-gu, Pusan
Tel: +82 (51) 633-3356; fax: +82 (51) 647-6132
Representative: Kim, Se-jung

Taeyoung Corporation (Water)
252-5, Gongdok-dong, Mapo-gu, Seoul
Tel: +82 (2) 3270-6999; fax: +82 (2) 719-1714
Representative: Byun, Tak

Sungwon Industry Development Co., Ltd. (Air, Water)
1008-4, Daechi 3-dong, Kangnam-gu, Seoul
Tel: +82 (2) 552-7777; fax: +82 (2) 3452-8981
Representative: Kim, Jong-mun

LG Engineering, Co., Ltd. (General)
537 Namdaemun-ro 5-ga, Chung-gu, Seoul
Tel: +82 (2) 728-3839; fax: +82 (2) 774-6610
Representative: Son, Ki-rak

Doosan Construction and Engineering (General)
105-7 Nonhyun-dong, Kangnam-gu, Seoul
Tel: +82 (2) 510-3114; fax: +82 (2) 511-5977
Representative: Min, Kyong-hoon

Daechang Enterprise Co., Ltd. (Water)
541, Namdaemunro 5-ga, Chung-gu, Seoul
Tel: +82 (2) 310-5700; fax: +82 (2) 310-5719
Representative: Lee, Jun

Dong-Ah Construction Industrial Co., Ltd. (General)
120-23 Seosomun-dong, Chung-gu, Seoul
Tel: +82 (2) 3709-2114; fax: +82 (2) 3709-3820
Representative: Koh, Byoung-woo

Daeho Corporation
1462-7, Seocho-dong, Seocho-ku, Seoul
Tel: +82 (2) 587-1853; fax: +82 (2) 587-1321
Representative: Kim, Sung-hoon

Hyundai Engineering and Construction Co., Ltd.
(General)
140-2 Kye-dong, Chongro-gu, Seoul
Tel: +82 (2) 746-2652; fax: +82 (2) 746-3122
Representative: Kim, Yun-kyu

Daelim Engineering Co., Ltd. (General)
23-9 Yoido-ding, Youngdungpo-gu, Seoul
Tel: +82 (2) 368-7114; fax: +82 (2) 368-6837
Representative: Lee, Jeong-guk

Samboo Construction Co., Ltd. (Water)
9-1 Namchang-dong, Chung-gu, Seoul
Tel: +82 (2) 752-9718; fax: +82 (2) 752-9718

Hyundai Precision and Industry Co., Ltd. (General)
140-2 Kye-dong, Chongro-gu, Seoul
Tel: +82 (2) 746-4081; fax: +82 (2) 746-3559
Representative: Park, Jeong-in

Dongbu Corporation (General)
838 Yoksam-dong, Kangnam-gu, Seoul
Tel: +82 (2) 262-2114; fax: +82 (2) 3484-2357
Representative: Baek, Ho-ik

Samhwan Enterprise Co., Ltd. (General)
98-20 Unni-dong, Chongro-gu, Seoul
Tel: +82 (2) 765-0151; fax: +82 (2) 740-2439

**Hyundai Industry Development and Construction Co.,
Ltd.** (General)
87 Samsung-dong, Kangnam-gu, Seoul
Tel: +82 (2) 519-9341
Representative: Chung, Mong-kyu

Lotte Engineering Co., Ltd. (General)
104 Wonhyoro 1-ga, Yongsan-gu, Seoul
Tel: +82 (2) 3270-0407; fax: +82 (2) 3270-0380
Representative: Kim, Woo-ryon

Limkwang Construction Co., Ltd. (General)
267 Migeun-dong, Sodaemun-gu, Seoul
Tel: +82 (2) 360-5052; fax: +82 (2) 360-5099
Representative: Lim, Jae-won

Speco Co., Ltd. (Air)
544-5 Dogok-dong, Kangnam-gu, Seoul
Tel: +82 (2) 3498-3264; fax: +82 (2) 3463-3645
Representative: Kim, Jong-seop

Korea Cottrel Co., Ltd. (Air)
160-1 Donggyo-dong, Mapo-gu, Seoul
Tel: +82 (2) 320-6114; fax: +82 (2) 320-6100
Representative: Lee, Tae-young

Kyungnam Enterprise Co., Ltd. (General)
34-3 Yoido-dong, Youngdungpo-gu, Seoul
Tel: +82 (2) 768-4536; fax: +82 (2) 768-4799
Representative: Cho, Byung-soo

Hanhwa Corporation (General)
1 Changgyo-dong, Chung-gu, Seoul
Tel: +82 (2) 729-1552; fax: +82 (2) 729-2305
Representative: Choi, Sang-soon

Wonbang Tech Co., Ltd. (Noise and Vibration)
2-44 Yangjae-dong, Seocho-gu, Seoul
Tel: +82 (2) 577-9031; fax: +82 (2) 577-2832
Representative: Im, Jae-min

Manufacturers/Distributors of Environmental Products

Blue Wales Clean
878-2 Kwanyang-dong, Dongan-gu, Anyang-shi, Kyonggi-do
Tel: +82 (31) 422-8700; fax: +82 (31) 422-8048
Product: filter for wastewater treatment

O-Three Tech Co., Ltd.
Bicenter #102, 1893 Shindang-dong, Dalseo-gu, Taegu
Tel: +82 (53) 586-9251; fax: +82 (53) 586-9253
Product: ozone analyzer

Saehan Environmental Technology Co., Ltd.
554-2, Kuro 5-dong, Kuro-gu, Seoul
Tel: +82 (2) 851-2508; fax: +82 (2) 851-2509
Products: dust collector, incinerator

Dongmun Science
923, Mok 1-dong, Yangchon-gu, Seoul
Tel: +82 (2) 2649-3891; fax: +82 (2) 2649-3890
Product: water analyzer

Youngin Science
547 Shinsa-dong, Kangnam-gu, Seoul
Tel: +82 (2) 519-7300; fax: +82 (2) 517-7400
Products: environmental chemicals, measuring and analyzing instruments

Youngshin Engineering
494-14 Yonggang-dong, Mapo-gu, Seoul
Tel: +82 (2) 3272-8567
Product: road cleaning vehicles

Donghoo Logistics Co., Ltd.
394-41 Shindorim-dong, Kuro-gu, Seoul
Tel: +82 (2) 672-2131; fax: +82 (2) 676-8589
Product: level indicator

Hyosung Evara Environmental Engineering
53-5, Wonhyoro 3-ga, Yongsan-gu, Seoul
Tel: +82 (2) 3271-7114; fax: +82 (2) 3271-7117
Product: wastewater treatment equipment

Hwachun Machinery Industry Co., Ltd.
1022-7 Bangbae-dong, Seocho-gu, Seoul
Tel: +82 (2) 523-7766; fax: +82 (2) 523-2867
Product: municipal sewage treatment equipment

Koryo Incineration Industry Co., Ltd.
Lot 3, Block 127, Namdong Export Industrial Park, Kojan-dong, Namdong-gu, Inchon
Tel: +82 (32) 817-5100; fax: +82 (32) 813-0077
Product: incinerators

J.O. Tech Co., Ltd.
5305, Wonhyoro 3-ga, Yongsan-gu, Seoul
Tel: +82 (31) 988-4296; fax: +82 (31) 988-1738
Product: measuring instruments

Samkyung Chemicals
255-5, Eulchi-ro 4-ga, Chung-gu, Seoul
Tel: +82 (2) 2277-2617; fax: +82 (2) 2265-2875
Contact: Hong, Chang-gi, President
Product: environmental chemicals

Woojin Environmental Industry Co., Ltd.
929-1 Wolam-dong, Dalseo-gu, Taegu
Tel: +82 (53) 582 4711; fax: +82 (53) 582-4716
Product: clean incinerator

Young Engineering Co., Ltd.
Yanggyong Building 501, 386-2 Mangwon-dong, Mapo-gu, Seoul
Tel: +82 (2) 326-0762; fax: +82 (2) 326-0761
Product: incinerators

Bando Machinery Co., Ltd.
409-3 Songnae-dong, Sosa-gu, Buchon-shi, Kyonggi-do
Tel: +82 (32) 666-3701; fax: +82 (32) 652-0351
Product: creep hoists

Korea OVAL Co., Ltd.
34 Yoido-dong, Youngdungpo-gu, Seoul
Tel: +82 (2) 783-2065; fax: +82 (2) 784-4303
Product: flow control systems

Sungji Industry
Kumho Building 3rd Floor, 123-25 Karak-dong, Songpa-gu,
Seoul
Tel: +82 (2) 400-7916; fax: +82 (2) 431-2570
Product: fume remover

Environmental Machinery Industry Co., Ltd.
1217-8 Jeongwang-dong, Shiheung-shi, Kyonggi-do
Tel: +82 (31) 499-9800; fax: +82 (31) 499-9809
Product: dust collector

Yukong Yuche Industry Co., Ltd.
944-2 Shinjong-dong, Yangchon-gu, Seoul
Tel: +82 (2) 695-7173; fax: +82 (2) 694-7105
Product: diaphragm valves for bag filters

Chongro Instruments
97-1, Kumhodong 4-ga, Seongdong-gu, Seoul
Tel: +82 (2) 297-9900; fax: +82 (2) 298-6419
Product: water quality measuring instruments

Unison Industry Co., Ltd.
1306-3 Seocho-dong, Seocho-gu, Seoul
Tel: +82 (2) 553-9161; fax: +82 (2) 553-6415
Product: drying and incineration systems